RONALD REAGAN

RONALD REAGAN

Renée Schwartzberg

CHELSEA HOUSE PUBLISHERS
NEW YORK
PHILADELPHIA

Chelsea House Publishers
EDITOR-IN-CHIEF: Remmel Nunn
MANAGING EDITOR: Karyn Gullen Browne
COPY CHIEF: Juliann Barbato
PICTURE EDITOR: Adrian G. Allen
ART DIRECTOR: Maria Epes
DEPUTY COPY CHIEF: Mark Rifkin
ASSISTANT ART DIRECTOR: Noreen Romano
MANUFACTURING MANAGER: Gerald Levine
SYSTEMS MANAGER: Lindsey Ottman
PRODUCTION MANAGER: Joseph Romano
PRODUCTION COORDINATOR: Marie Claire Cebrián

World Leaders—Past & Present
SENIOR EDITOR: John W. Selfridge

Staff for RONALD REAGAN
COPY EDITOR: Joseph Roman
EDITORIAL ASSISTANT: Martin Mooney
PICTURE RESEARCHER: Sandy Jones
DESIGNER: David Murray
ASSISTANT DESIGNER: Diana Blume
COVER ILLUSTRATION: Bryn Barnard

First Printing

1 3 5 7 9 8 6 4 2

Library of Congress Cataloging-in-Publication Data

Schwartzberg, Renée.
  Ronald Reagan/Renée Schwartzberg.
  p. cm.—(World leaders—past and present)
  Includes bibliographical references and index.
  Summary: A biography of the first movie-star president, with
photos, captions, and quotes.
  ISBN 1-55546-849-7
     0-7910-0684-0 (pbk.)
  1. Reagan, Ronald—Juvenile literature. 2. Presidents—United
States—Biography—Juvenile literature. [1. Reagan, Ronald.
2. Presidents. 3. Actors and actresses.] I. Title. II. Series: World
leaders past & present.
E877.S25 1991
973.927′092   90-35961
[B]   CIP
[92]   AC

Contents

John Adams
John Quincy Adams
Konrad Adenauer
Alexander the Great
Salvador Allende
Marc Antony
Corazon Aquino
Yasir Arafat
King Arthur
Hafez al-Assad
Kemal Atatürk
Attila
Clement Attlee
Augustus Caesar
Menachem Begin
David Ben-Gurion
Otto von Bismarck
Léon Blum
Simon Bolívar
Cesare Borgia
Willy Brandt
Leonid Brezhnev
Julius Caesar
John Calvin
Jimmy Carter
Fidel Castro
Catherine the Great
Charlemagne
Chiang Kai-Shek
Winston Churchill
Georges Clemenceau
Cleopatra
Constantine the Great
Hernán Cortés
Oliver Cromwell
Georges-Jacques
   Danton
Jefferson Davis
Moshe Dayan
Charles de Gaulle
Eamon De Valera
Eugene Debs
Deng Xiaoping
Benjamin Disraeli
Alexander Dubček
François & Jean-Claude
   Duvalier
Dwight Eisenhower
Eleanor of Aquitaine
Elizabeth I
Faisal
Ferdinand & Isabella
Francisco Franco
Benjamin Franklin

Frederick the Great
Indira Gandhi
Mohandas Gandhi
Giuseppe Garibaldi
Amin & Bashir Gemayel
Genghis Khan
William Gladstone
Mikhail Gorbachev
Ulysses S. Grant
Ernesto "Che" Guevara
Tenzin Gyatso
Alexander Hamilton
Dag Hammarskjöld
Henry VIII
Henry of Navarre
Paul von Hindenburg
Hirohito
Adolf Hitler
Ho Chi Minh
King Hussein
Ivan the Terrible
Andrew Jackson
James I
Wojciech Jaruzelski
Thomas Jefferson
Joan of Arc
Pope John XXIII
Pope John Paul II
Lyndon Johnson
Benito Juárez
John Kennedy
Robert Kennedy
Jomo Kenyatta
Ayatollah Khomeini
Nikita Khrushchev
Kim Il Sung
Martin Luther King, Jr.
Henry Kissinger
Kublai Khan
Lafayette
Robert E. Lee
Vladimir Lenin
Abraham Lincoln
David Lloyd George
Louis XIV
Martin Luther
Judas Maccabeus
James Madison
Nelson & Winnie
   Mandela
Mao Zedong
Ferdinand Marcos
George Marshall

Mary, Queen of Scots
Tomáš Masaryk
Golda Meir
Klemens von Metternich
James Monroe
Hosni Mubarak
Robert Mugabe
Benito Mussolini
Napoléon Bonaparte
Gamal Abdel Nasser
Jawaharlal Nehru
Nero
Nicholas II
Richard Nixon
Kwame Nkrumah
Daniel Ortega
Mohammed Reza Pahlavi
Thomas Paine
Charles Stewart
   Parnell
Pericles
Juan Perón
Peter the Great
Pol Pot
Muammar el-Qaddafi
Ronald Reagan
Cardinal Richelieu
Maximilien Robespierre
Eleanor Roosevelt
Franklin Roosevelt
Theodore Roosevelt
Anwar Sadat
Haile Selassie
Prince Sihanouk
Jan Smuts
Joseph Stalin
Sukarno
Sun Yat-sen
Tamerlane
Mother Teresa
Margaret Thatcher
Josip Broz Tito
Toussaint L'Ouverture
Leon Trotsky
Pierre Trudeau
Harry Truman
Queen Victoria
Lech Walesa
George Washington
Chaim Weizmann
Woodrow Wilson
Xerxes
Emiliano Zapata
Zhou Enlai

CHELSEA HOUSE PUBLISHERS

ON LEADERSHIP

Arthur M. Schlesinger, jr.

LEADERSHIP, it may be said, is really what makes the world go round. Love no doubt smooths the passage; but love is a private transaction between consenting adults. Leadership is a public transaction with history. The idea of leadership affirms the capacity of individuals to move, inspire, and mobilize masses of people so that they act together in pursuit of an end. Sometimes leadership serves good purposes, sometimes bad; but whether the end is benign or evil, great leaders are those men and women who leave their personal stamp on history.

Now, the very concept of leadership implies the proposition that individuals can make a difference. This proposition has never been universally accepted. From classical times to the present day, eminent thinkers have regarded individuals as no more than the agents and pawns of larger forces, whether the gods and goddesses of the ancient world or, in the modern era, race, class, nation, the dialectic, the will of the people, the spirit of the times, history itself. Against such forces, the individual dwindles into insignificance.

So contends the thesis of historical determinism. Tolstoy's great novel *War and Peace* offers a famous statement of the case. Why, Tolstoy asked, did millions of men in the Napoleonic Wars, denying their human feelings and their common sense, move back and forth across Europe slaughtering their fellows? "The war," Tolstoy answered, "was bound to happen simply because it was bound to happen." All prior history predetermined it. As for leaders, they, Tolstoy said, "are but the labels that serve to give a name to an end and, like labels, they have the least possible connection with the event." The greater the leader, "the more conspicuous the inevitability and the predestination of every act he commits." The leader, said Tolstoy, is "the slave of history."

Determinism takes many forms. Marxism is the determinism of class. Nazism the determinism of race. But the idea of men and women as the slaves of history runs athwart the deepest human instincts. Rigid determinism abolishes the idea of human freedom—

the assumption of free choice that underlies every move we make, every word we speak, every thought we think. It abolishes the idea of human responsibility, since it is manifestly unfair to reward or punish people for actions that are by definition beyond their control. No one can live consistently by any deterministic creed. The Marxist states prove this themselves by their extreme susceptibility to the cult of leadership.

More than that, history refutes the idea that individuals make no difference. In December 1931 a British politician crossing Park Avenue in New York City between 76th and 77th Streets around 10:30 P.M. looked in the wrong direction and was knocked down by an automobile—a moment, he later recalled, of a man aghast, a world aglare: "I do not understand why I was not broken like an eggshell or squashed like a gooseberry." Fourteen months later an American politician, sitting in an open car in Miami, Florida, was fired on by an assassin; the man beside him was hit. Those who believe that individuals make no difference to history might well ponder whether the next two decades would have been the same had Mario Constasino's car killed Winston Churchill in 1931 and Giuseppe Zangara's bullet killed Franklin Roosevelt in 1933. Suppose, in addition, that Adolf Hitler had been killed in the street fighting during the Munich *Putsch* of 1923 and that Lenin had died of typhus during World War I. What would the 20th century be like now?

For better or for worse, individuals do make a difference. "The notion that a people can run itself and its affairs anonymously," wrote the philosopher William James, "is now well known to be the silliest of absurdities. Mankind does nothing save through initiatives on the part of inventors, great or small, and imitation by the rest of us—these are the sole factors in human progress. Individuals of genius show the way, and set the patterns, which common people then adopt and follow."

Leadership, James suggests, means leadership in thought as well as in action. In the long run, leaders in thought may well make the greater difference to the world. But, as Woodrow Wilson once said, "Those only are leaders of men, in the general eye, who lead in action. . . . It is at their hands that new thought gets its translation into the crude language of deeds." Leaders in thought often invent in solitude and obscurity, leaving to later generations the tasks of imitation. Leaders in action—the leaders portrayed in this series—have to be effective in their own time.

And they cannot be effective by themselves. They must act in response to the rhythms of their age. Their genius must be adapted, in a phrase of William James's, "to the receptivities of the moment." Leaders are useless without followers. "There goes the mob," said the French politician hearing a clamor in the streets. "I am their leader. I must follow them." Great leaders turn the inchoate emotions of the mob to purposes of their own. They seize on the opportunities of their time, the hopes, fears, frustrations, crises, potentialities. They succeed when events have prepared the way for them, when the community is awaiting to be aroused, when they can provide the clarifying and organizing ideas. Leadership ignites the circuit between the individual and the mass and thereby alters history.

It may alter history for better or for worse. Leaders have been responsible for the most extravagant follies and most monstrous crimes that have beset suffering humanity. They have also been vital in such gains as humanity has made in individual freedom, religious and racial tolerance, social justice, and respect for human rights.

There is no sure way to tell in advance who is going to lead for good and who for evil. But a glance at the gallery of men and women in *World Leaders—Past and Present* suggests some useful tests.

One test is this: Do leaders lead by force or by persuasion? By command or by consent? Through most of history leadership was exercised by the divine right of authority. The duty of followers was to defer and to obey. "Theirs not to reason why / Theirs but to do and die." On occasion, as with the so-called enlightened despots of the 18th century in Europe, absolutist leadership was animated by humane purposes. More often, absolutism nourished the passion for domination, land, gold, and conquest and resulted in tyranny.

The great revolution of modern times has been the revolution of equality. The idea that all people should be equal in their legal condition has undermined the old structure of authority, hierarchy, and deference. The revolution of equality has had two contrary effects on the nature of leadership. For equality, as Alexis de Tocqueville pointed out in his great study *Democracy in America*, might mean equality in servitude as well as equality in freedom.

"I know of only two methods of establishing equality in the political world," Tocqueville wrote. "Rights must be given to every citizen, or none at all to anyone . . . save one, who is the master of all." There was no middle ground "between the sovereignty of all and the absolute power of one man." In his astonishing prediction of 20th-century totalitarian dictatorship, Tocqueville explained how the revolution of equality could lead to the *"Führerprinzip"* and more terrible absolutism than the world had ever known.

But when rights are given to every citizen and the sovereignty of all is established, the problem of leadership takes a new form, becomes more exacting than ever before. It is easy to issue commands and enforce them by the rope and the stake, the concentration camp and the *gulag.* It is much harder to use argument and achievement to overcome opposition and win consent. The Founding Fathers of the United States understood the difficulty. They believed that history had given them the opportunity to decide, as Alexander Hamilton wrote in the first Federalist Paper, whether men are indeed capable of basing government on "reflection and choice, or whether they are forever destined to depend . . . on accident and force."

Government by reflection and choice called for a new style of leadership and a new quality of followership. It required leaders to be responsive to popular concerns, and it required followers to be active and informed participants in the process. Democracy does not eliminate emotion from politics; sometimes it fosters demagoguery; but it is confident that, as the greatest of democratic leaders put it, you cannot fool all of the people all of the time. It measures leadership by results and retires those who overreach or falter or fail.

It is true that in the long run despots are measured by results too. But they can postpone the day of judgment, sometimes indefinitely, and in the meantime they can do infinite harm. It is also true that democracy is no guarantee of virtue and intelligence in government, for the voice of the people is not necessarily the voice of God. But democracy, by assuring the right of opposition, offers built-in resistance to the evils inherent in absolutism. As the theologian Reinhold Niebuhr summed it up, "Man's capacity for justice makes democracy possible, but man's inclination to injustice makes democracy necessary."

A second test for leadership is the end for which power is sought. When leaders have as their goal the supremacy of a master race or the promotion of totalitarian revolution or the acquisition and exploitation of colonies or the protection of greed and privilege or the preservation of personal power, it is likely that their leadership will do little to advance the cause of humanity. When their goal is the abolition of slavery, the liberation of women, the enlargement of opportunity for the poor and powerless, the extension of equal rights to racial minorities, the defense of the freedoms of expression and opposition, it is likely that their leadership will increase the sum of human liberty and welfare.

Leaders have done great harm to the world. They have also conferred great benefits. You will find both sorts in this series. Even "good" leaders must be regarded with a certain wariness. Leaders are not demigods; they put on their trousers one leg after another just like ordinary mortals. No leader is infallible, and every leader needs to be reminded of this at regular intervals. Irreverence irritates leaders but is their salvation. Unquestioning submission corrupts leaders and demeans followers. Making a cult of a leader is always a mistake. Fortunately hero worship generates its own antidote. "Every hero," said Emerson, "becomes a bore at last."

The signal benefit the great leaders confer is to embolden the rest of us to live according to our own best selves, to be active, insistent, and resolute in affirming our own sense of things. For great leaders attest to the reality of human freedom against the supposed inevitabilities of history. And they attest to the wisdom and power that may lie within the most unlikely of us, which is why Abraham Lincoln remains the supreme example of great leadership. A great leader, said Emerson, exhibits new possibilities to all humanity. "We feed on genius. . . . Great men exist that there may be greater men."

Great leaders, in short, justify themselves by emancipating and empowering their followers. So humanity struggles to master its destiny, remembering with Alexis de Tocqueville: "It is true that around every man a fatal circle is traced beyond which he cannot pass; but within the wide verge of that circle he is powerful and free; as it is with man, so with communities."

1

Reykjavík 1986

In what might have been a prelude to a great historical moment, Ronald Wilson Reagan and Mikhail
Sergeyevich Gorbachev — the president of the United
States and the premier of the Union of Soviet Socialist Republics — met in Reykjavík, Iceland, in October 1986. It was not their first meeting — that had
been the previous November, in Geneva, Switzerland — but now there was greater urgency in their
efforts to achieve a breakthrough on the issue of
arms reduction. This hastily arranged, unofficial
summit in Reykjavík was another step in an ongoing process of nuclear arms negotiations between
the superpowers.

The United States and the Soviet Union had been
deadly enemies for more than 40 years and had
amassed vast stores of weapons with which to defend themselves, threaten each other, and advance
their respective global interests. Both Reagan and
Gorbachev had cut their political teeth as warriors
in the cold war.

> *Foreign policy wasn't terribly
> important to the president. He
> was defensive about foreign
> policy, didn't know a lot about
> it himself.*
> —ROBERT MCFARLANE
> Reagan's national
> security adviser

**Soviet leader Mikhail Gorbachev (left) and U.S. president
Ronald Reagan (right) meet in Reykjavík, Iceland, in October 1986. At the summit, Gorbachev made dramatic
proposals for arms reduction that took the Americans by
surprise.**

Still, both leaders were eager to sign an arms agreement for political reasons. A little more than a year after becoming general secretary of the Communist party in the Soviet Union, Gorbachev — at 55 the youngest person to hold that position in 50 years — wanted to end the arms race in order to conserve his country's resources and to enable him to concentrate on solving the Soviet Union's dire domestic problems. With the Soviet economy in a shambles and popular discontent reaching dangerous proportions throughout the Soviet Union, Gorbachev sought to strengthen his image at home as well as in the international sphere.

Reagan — at 75 the oldest American president ever — was halfway through his second and final term, and many were calling him the most successful U.S. president since World War II. The American economy was strong, and he enjoyed enormous popularity at home. Still, Reagan and his party, the Republicans, believed that a significant arms reduction agreement was necessary to assure his place in history not only as a great American president but also as an accomplished international statesman.

The two leaders were unlikely comrades. Gorbachev, a trained lawyer, had diligently worked his way through the ranks of the Communist party before attaining the position of general secretary in May 1985. With a prominent, maplike birthmark on his bald head, with his gray suits, medium height, and solid build, Gorbachev looked the part of a shrewd, polished professional. A smart public relations manager, able to think and act quickly even when under great pressure, Gorbachev easily charmed the masses, both at home and abroad, with his smile and his wit. Compared to the dull Soviet bureaucrats who had preceded him, Gorbachev was warm, dynamic, and open minded — a true man of the people. Sharp, agile, knowledgeable, and energetic, he was an unabashed reformer who had already begun making changes that would lead, with incredible speed, to a complete realignment of the world's political order by the end of the decade.

Not surprisingly, Gorbachev greeted his American counterpart in Reykjavík with innovative, dramatic, even startling arms proposals.

Like Gorbachev, Reagan was a persuasive speaker who won over the masses with his warmth and good nature, but his brand of charisma was distinct from that of his Soviet counterpart. Tall and rugged, dressed often in cowboy boots and brown suits with heavily padded shoulders, Reagan, though in his seventies, had a full head of dark hair, which he claimed he never dyed. His rough-and-ready yet friendly and self-deprecating cowboy persona, which he had cultivated with great success ever since he was a young man, had helped make him a leading figure in the Republican party for more than 20 years. Whereas Gorbachev had spent virtually his entire life preparing for a career in government, Reagan had had no such training. Hailing from a small town in Illinois, he had been a sportscaster, a television and Hollywood movie actor, a union president, and a corporate spokesman before becoming governor of California. After serving two terms as California's chief administrator, Reagan was elected president of the United States in November 1980 and reelected in 1984.

Both Gorbachev and Reagan may be viewed as reformers, but whereas the Soviet leader sought to push his country forward toward a better way of life with proposals based on new ideas, Reagan preferred old ones. The rise to power of Ronald Reagan represented a "revolution of the Right," a reform movement based on a firm belief in free enterprise, staunch anticommunism, and traditional values. The movement sought to bring back the simple, wholesome life of a bygone era, when the supporting pillars of American society — church and family — were unshakable.

An avid, almost visceral anti-Communist, and the moving force behind an unprecedented American military buildup, Reagan seemed the least likely president to join the Soviets in reducing the number of nuclear warheads that the superpowers had aimed at one another and at each other's allies. Yet,

Only a year before the Reykjavík summit, Reagan and Gorbachev met in Geneva, Switzerland, to discuss a possible arms treaty between the United States and the Soviet Union. Here, Reagan gestures to his Soviet counterpart as U.S. chief of staff Donald Regan (center) closely observes.

Ronald Reagan eagerly sat down at the negotiating table in Reykjavík, Iceland, in October 1986 to discuss nuclear arms reduction.

Reagan had gone to Geneva a year before in an attempt to boost his approval ratings in the polls at home and to establish a personal rapport with the Soviet leader. He had great faith in his persuasiveness, his influence over others, one-on-one. But, in fact, Reagan one-on-one was a pushover. No matter how firm and stern he might be on public policy issues abstractly, when faced with an individual's problems and needs, he was invariably more responsive than assertive.

Since his days in Hollywood, Reagan had usually followed a script, rarely if ever improvising. But the meeting in Reykjavík had not been scripted in advance. It was intended merely to smooth the way for an official summit later that year in Moscow. No new initiatives were expected. Gorbachev's daring new proposals surprised Reagan and forced him to improvise. That put Gorbachev at a great advantage because Reagan, not well versed in nuclear weapons technology, was unprepared to deal with the substantive issues. Consequently, he followed the Soviet leader's initiative. Their respective teams of negotiators worked through the night on more drastic reductions of nuclear arms than had ever been seriously considered.

By October 13, the way had been cleared for the elimination of all ballistic missiles, which Reagan had never intended. Though he knew little about nuclear weapons and the arms race, he did know that with both sides shorn of nuclear weapons, the Soviet Union — with superior conventional armed forces in Eastern Europe — would have the military advantage over the United States and its allies. Reagan, who had built his entire career on the fear instilled in Americans by the threat of Soviet military superiority, had made an egregious error. How had this happened?

Unfamiliar with the terminology used in superpower arms negotiations, Reagan misunderstood the word *ballistic*, which is a term that may be used to describe all nuclear missiles. Reagan thought the word referred to a single class of weapons, such as intermediate-range or land-based missiles, rather than naming a category that included all of these. Thus, Reagan thought that by agreeing to eliminate ballistic missiles he was agreeing to scrap only a certain kind of nuclear missile; actually, he was offering to dismantle the entire U.S. nuclear arsenal. Only his intransigeance on SDI — the Strategic Defense Initiative — saved Reagan from catastrophe at Reykjavík.

SDI was the Reagan administration's boldest defense program. In a televised speech on March 23, 1983, Reagan proposed the creation of a complex

> *The fact that nobody anticipated that the Soviets were going to put a deal on the table, and that Reagan wasn't given an alternative strategy just in case, was criminal—absolutely criminal.*
> —MICHAEL DEAVER
> former Reagan aide, on the Reykjavík summit

17

system of high-tech land- and space-based weapons that would destroy incoming missiles before they reached their targets. In Reagan's vision — popularly known as "Star Wars" — SDI would end forever the threat of nuclear annihilation.

Most scientists agreed, however, that SDI provided an extremely optimistic, in fact unrealistic, picture of the future and was severely flawed. SDI depended on advanced devices, including laser weapons, which did not exist, and on millions of lines of computer code. Even the simplest computer programs need extensive debugging — correction of errors — before they will operate successfully. The unprecedentedly complicated SDI computer programs could never be debugged properly until put to the test of an actual exchange of nuclear missiles. Mistakes could not be discovered until it was too late.

Discounting the questionable viability of an impenetrable shield, SDI raised other significant issues — staggering costs (an estimated $100 to $200 billion a year for at least 10 years) and destabilization. Besides violating the long-standing treaty covering antiballistic missiles (ABMs), an agreement prohibiting antinuclear defenses, SDI technology could conceivably be used offensively. Reagan had pledged to share SDI, but the Soviets considered it a threat to world peace that would only escalate the arms race. SDI was the sticking point at Reykjavík. After agreeing to eliminate ballistic missiles, Reagan continued to insist on the right to proceed with SDI development and deployment — at which point his negotiations with Gorbachev collapsed.

The two leaders left Reykjavík on very bad terms, replete with mutual recriminations — each blaming the other for their failure — and with no clear notion of when, or if, they would meet again. Instead of easing tensions and paving the way for a great moment in history, the meeting at Reykjavík seemed to have ruined any chance of improving relations between the superpowers during what little remained of Reagan's presidency.

Those in the Reagan administration charged with manipulating the press by putting the best face on

Some of us are like a shovel brigade that follows a parade down Main Street cleaning up. We took Reykjavik and turned what was really a sour situation into something that turned out pretty well.
—DONALD REGAN
Reagan's chief of staff

even the worst occurrences — so-called spin doctors — attempted to tack a veneer over the Reykjavík debacle. They tried to portray Reagan as both flexible and hard nosed, explaining his acceptance of ballistic missile elimination by saying the president was speaking of total elimination as an ultimate objective to be attained at some distant time in the future. Moreover, the spin doctors tried to placate those in the press who criticized Reagan for not being firm enough with Gorbachev by underscoring the president's hard-line position on SDI. Still, no amount of spin control could deny that the Reagan administration had failed terribly at Reykjavík, and many viewed the affair as one more episode in a troubled and seemingly incompetent administration. History will ultimately judge.

Gorbachev and Reagan chat during the Reykjavík summit. When Reagan returned to Washington, his handlers tried to put the best face on the failure of the Reykjavík meeting, but expectations had been so high and the results so disappointing that the spin doctors were unable to gloss over the reality.

2
California Here I Come

Ronald Reagan was born on February 6, 1911, in an apartment above the general store in which his father, John Edward Reagan, was employed, in the small town of Tampico, Illinois. Jack, as his father was called, was a handsome and muscular Irish-American shoe salesman, proud of his diploma from the American School of Proctipedics. He was also a great storyteller. One of few Democrats in a predominantly Republican setting, and a rare Catholic among Protestants, Jack Reagan bequeathed to his son Ronald and to Ronald's older brother, Neil, his gift of gab.

Jack Reagan, who had once chosen to spend the night in his car rather than stay at a hotel that excluded Jews, strongly believed that racial discrimination was unjust. He instilled that same belief in his sons, whom he refused to let see D. W. Griffith's landmark motion picture, *Birth of a Nation*, because of its positive portrayal of the racist organization the Ku Klux Klan.

All in all, as I look back I realize that my reading left an abiding belief in the triumph of good over evil. There were heroes who lived by standards of morality and fair play.
—RONALD REAGAN
on his childhood influences

In a Reagan family portrait taken around 1913, John Edward Reagan and his wife, Nelle, pose with their children, Neil (left) and Ronald, who later described his childhood as "one of those rare Huck Finn–Tom Sawyer idylls."

Ronald Reagan's third grade class in Tampico, Illinois. Eight-year-old Ronald, or Dutch as he was called, is pictured in the second row at the far left.

Fortunately, the Reagan boys did not inherit their father's excessive drinking habit. When Ronald was 11 he found his father drunk and unconscious on the front porch. Not wanting his father to be seen in such a state, he struggled to drag him into the house. As he grew up, Ronald always remembered the incident and the powerful effect it had on him.

Ronald Reagan's aversion to alcohol was also partly a result of his mother's influence. Nelle Wilson Reagan, Ronald's mother, was of Scottish Presbyterian ancestry, but she had joined the Disciples of Christ, a Protestant sect that was at the forefront of an antialcohol temperance movement, and had brought Ronald into the group. The Disciples condemned those who used alcoholic beverages, but Nelle Reagan was a compassionate woman who asked her sons to love and help their father, who she believed was a good man simply unable to control his drinking. She also did volunteer work with the sick and the poor, and her example was a powerful one for her boys.

A determined self-improver, Nelle Reagan often took her family to lectures, musical recitals, and plays. Ronald Reagan would later refer to his mother as a frustrated actress because of her impromptu dialect performances and her writing and staging of morality plays for the Disciples. The future movie star's first stage appearances were made in his mother's skits.

Ronald Reagan — called "Dutch" because his father thought he looked like "a fat little Dutchman" as an infant — was much less outgoing than his older brother Neil — called "Moon" after the comic strip character, Moon Mullins. Small and extremely nearsighted, Ronald loved to draw and to play with toy soldiers, and he had a remarkable facility for memorization. He was impressed by the martian warlord stories of Tarzan creator Edgar Rice Burroughs, but the book that had the greatest impact on his adult life was Harold Bell Wright's *That Printer of Udell's*, in which the hero attends night school, marries a beautiful socialite, and blends Christian and business principles to improve his small midwestern town before finally becoming a congressman.

The Reagan family moved about Illinois frequently, taking up residence in Chicago, then in Tampico, then in Galesburg, and then in Dixon. In fact, they moved four times within the borders of Tampico and five times during their stay in Dixon, where the Reagans settled more or less permanently when Ronald was nine. Thus, at a very early age Ronald Reagan learned how to live out of a suitcase, important training for an aspiring young actor.

In 1924, when he was 13, Reagan entered Dixon's North Side High School. He was at best a middling student. Football mattered more to him than study. He earned a place on the football team and inspired his fellow players with his determination, not his skill.

Though not a great football player, Reagan was a powerful swimmer. For seven summers he worked as the lifeguard at Lowell Park, on the Rock River. It was a grueling job, demanding 12 hours a day, 7 days a week, every day of his summer vacations. There were dangerous undertows in the Rock River, and before his career as a lifeguard ended, Reagan had rescued 77 people from drowning, becoming, deservedly, a local hero.

Sports mattered a great deal to the young Reagan, who played for the North Side High School football team in Dixon, Illinois, during the 1920s. Though not an outstanding member of the squad, Reagan made up for his limited athletic ability with team spirit and determination.

Affable and popular, Reagan was elected student body president in his senior year at North Side High. He fell in love with Margaret "Muggs" Cleaver, daughter of the Disciples' minister, Reverend Ben Cleaver. Ronald and Muggs played the leads in a staging of Philip Barry's *You and I*, and he quickly won her affection. The romance would last eight years, and Reverend Cleaver would serve as a father figure to Reagan, advising him, helping him get into college, even teaching him how to drive a car.

In 1928, Reagan and Muggs enrolled at Eureka College, a Disciples school in Eureka, Illinois. Here, too, Reagan was primarily interested in football, although he majored in economics and sociology. Eureka was a small school with a small staff, and Reagan was still not much of a student. He usually studied only for exams, always at the last minute, and his photographic memory would make up for earlier failures of application. Reagan had a partial scholarship to Eureka, which he supplemented by working, mostly as a dishwasher.

During Reagan's freshman year, the underendowed institution suffered a budget crunch, and the college president sought to balance the budget by cutting courses and laying off faculty. The students, with faculty prodding, organized a strike, and Reagan became a student leader. Making his first political speech at a special midnight strike rally, Reagan gained his first taste of the power of oratory, his ability to move others to action with words. Promptly the cutback plans were abandoned.

At Eureka, the stage continued to fascinate Reagan. He played a shepherd who is strangled to death in Edna St. Vincent Millay's antiwar play, *Aria da Capo* (Reagan considered himself a pacifist then), and when the drama department entered this production in the prestigious one-act play competition at Northwestern University in Chicago, it took second place, and Reagan was cited for his acting.

This acting ability entertained his friends when Reagan made up mythical football games, "broadcasting" with a broomstick as if it were a microphone. But no one found it entertaining when the Eureka team, on the road, stopped at a hotel that refused to let the team's two black players enter. This was Reagan's first direct experience of racial prejudice, and he responded by taking the rejected players to spend the night at his parents' house.

During Reagan's sophomore year in 1930, the economically disastrous Great Depression struck. Jack Reagan lost his job, and Nelle Reagan found work in a dress shop. Ronald helped by sending $50 to his mother — secretly, so his father would not be embarrassed.

Jack Reagan played a prominent role in Dixon during Franklin Delano Roosevelt's campaign for president in 1932. When Roosevelt, a Democrat and governor of New York, became president, Jack Reagan was rewarded with control of the local welfare office. Neil Reagan also worked in the relief programs that were part of Roosevelt's New Deal, and Roosevelt became Ronald Reagan's hero. He listened regularly to Roosevelt's Fireside Chats on the radio and developed a convincing imitation of the president, memorizing long passages from Roosevelt's speeches.

By the time Reagan graduated from Eureka on June 7, 1932, he and Margaret Cleaver were engaged to be married. He went back to Dixon to work for a short time in the sporting goods department of the local Montgomery Ward store before returning to Lowell Park for his final summer as a lifeguard.

Reagan's former high school drama teacher, B. J. Frazer, suggested that he seek his future in communications, and Sid Altschuler, a wealthy Kansas City businessman who spent summers in Dixon, recommended that he take any job to get his foot in the door of the fledgling radio industry. While Reagan struggled to take this advice — spending months seeking employment at every radio station for miles around — Margaret Cleaver left Dixon to teach. Traveling in Europe the next year, she fell in love with another man and returned Reagan's engagement ring.

Reagan finally got a break at WOC, the "World of Chiropractic" radio station in Davenport, Iowa, performing so well as the announcer of University of Iowa football games that in early 1933, at the age

I went through a period in college, in the aftermath of World War I, where I became a pacifist and thought the whole thing was a frame-up.
—RONALD REAGAN
on his disillusionment as a college student

of 22, he received a regular announcer's position at the then-substantial salary of $25 a week. At first he was stymied by the requirement of reading advertisements over the air because he was not good at cold script readings. Realizing it would be better to memorize the script and rehearse it, he became a very persuasive salesman.

WOC and its sister station, WHO, consolidated operations, and Reagan was sent to Des Moines, Iowa, as a sports announcer, primarily to cover Chicago Cubs baseball. In those days, broadcast games were frequently re-created and dramatized by the announcers from terse pitch-by-pitch wire service accounts. Reagan once improvised his way out of a jam when the wire went dead by inventing a seemingly endless series of foul balls for the batter at the plate. Actually, the batter had popped out on the first pitch, but not in Reagan's account.

This improvisational ability proved useful one night when Reagan, at home, heard a nurse being assaulted in the street below. Daringly, he leaned out the window and frightened off the assailant by threatening to shoot him. Reagan had no gun.

During the 1930s, Reagan worked as a sportscaster for WHO radio in Des Moines, Iowa, covering the Chicago Cubs baseball team. Reagan greatly enjoyed his work in sports journalism, and many listeners appreciated his uniquely creative play-by-play style.

As Reagan became increasingly popular, his salary was raised to $75 a week. He socialized at Drake University with other Disciples, kept physically fit, and took up horseback riding. Enlisting as a reserve cavalry officer at Fort Des Moines, Reagan evinced no interest in military service. He just wanted a place to ride horses year-round.

By 1936, his salary had reached $90 a week, most of which he saved to buy a new car — a Nash convertible. By now a six-footer, Reagan was a notable sight, cruising around town with the top down. His face grew to be as familiar as his voice as he became a frequent speaker on civic occasions, an attraction at the state fair, and a sports columnist for the *Des Moines Dispatch*.

When Gene Autry, the Hollywood cowboy star, signed WHO musicians to appear in a movie, Reagan — who had never lost his taste for acting — began to think he too might make it in movies. With the intention of seeking his fortune in Hollywood, Reagan persuaded the station to send him to Los Angeles to cover the Cubs' spring training in 1937.

Before leaving for Los Angeles, Reagan was introduced to a local girl who had had some success in Hollywood. She, in turn, introduced him to her agent, Bill Meiklejohn, who was convinced he could make Reagan the next Robert Taylor, who was then an extremely popular leading man. Reagan lied about his experience, claiming that the Eureka Drama Club was a professional stock company and that he earned $180 a week, and Meiklejohn got him a screen test with Warner Brothers casting director Max Arnow. Arnow tested Reagan in the appropriate role of an earnest young man and signed him to a 6-month contract with an option to renew, at $200 a week.

WHO sponsor General Mills so appreciated Reagan's radio appearances that they made him a counteroffer, but Reagan was determined to make a life for himself in the movies. At the age of 26, he left Des Moines, so popular that his farewell party was broadcast. Even the mayor showed up to wish him well in Hollywood.

Life is just one grand sweet song, so start the music.
—quote below Reagan's name in his high school yearbook

3

Hooray for Hollywood

Hollywood was good to Reagan from the day he arrived at the Warner studio in Burbank, California, in June 1937. In September he brought his parents to live nearby, and three of his Drake University friends followed him west. Disciples of Christ formed Reagan's first circle of friends in Hollywood.

In his film debut, Reagan played a radio announcer in the movie *Love Is on the Air*. Reagan learned his scripts easily, took direction readily, and accepted unquestioningly the roles the studio selected, most typically as best friend of the film's leading man. Warner Brothers appreciated Reagan's talents, and the actor was given regular work in the B-picture division, providing second features for the double bills then usual in movie theaters. He made 7 other films during his first year in Hollywood, and within 2 years he made 16 films. The most significant of these to him personally was *Brother Rat*. He played only a small part, but during the filming in 1938, Reagan met Jane Wyman.

One measure of Reagan's ability as an actor is that he frequently won praise in films panned by the critics.
—LOU CANNON
Reagan biographer

Handsome, affable, Ronald Reagan was a big hit as a radio announcer, and gradually he enjoyed celebrity status throughout the Midwest. Then, inspired by the work of the western film star Gene Autry, Reagan set out for Hollywood in 1937 to pursue a movie career.

After seeing the movie *Knute Rockne, All American*, in which Reagan starred as the renowned football player George Gipp, art students at the University of Southern California invited the young actor to model for their sculpting class. Reagan, they said, had a nearly perfect male physique.

Reagan's romance with Jane Wyman was encouraged by gossip columnist Louella Parsons, who had noticed the handsome young actor when he played a small role in *Hollywood Hotel*, the film version of her radio program, "Cavalcade of Stars." Gossip columnists were very powerful in the Hollywood of the 1930s, and Parsons was attracted to Reagan because she too had grown up in Dixon, Illinois.

Parsons included Reagan in a star-studded visit to Dixon, where he, still remembered as a hero, received the warmest welcome. When Parsons put together a vaudeville-style touring show in 1939, Reagan was master of ceremonies and Wyman a "star of tomorrow." The Reagan-Wyman engagement was announced first on stage and then in Parsons's column.

Even before the wedding on January 26, 1940, the romance was treated in the press and by Warner's publicity department as a grand Hollywood story. The Reagans were idealized as a perfect couple, and countless envious onlookers declared that their marriage was made in heaven.

The couple spent their honeymoon in Palm Springs and then moved into Wyman's Beverly Hills apartment. Reagan continued starring in the Brass Bancroft series about a Treasury Department agent, or T-man. In the early movies, Bancroft battled counterfeiters, but the 1940 film *Murder in the Air* foreshadowed President Reagan's Strategic Defense Initiative with its "Inertia Projector," an airborne death ray that could knock down enemy airplanes before they dropped their bombs. This secret weapon would make America invincible and — in terms strikingly similar to those Reagan would later use to describe SDI — was called "the greatest force for world peace ever discovered."

Usually, Reagan simply took the roles he was offered, but there was one role he actively sought — that of football player George Gipp in *Knute Rockne, All American* — going so far as to show the casting director a picture of himself in his football uniform to prove he could look the part. Knute Rockne was the famous football coach of Notre Dame who had once used the mystique of Gipp — a standout runner who had died of pneumonia during the football season — to inspire his team to victory. "Let's win one for the Gipper" became a significant catchphrase during many of Reagan's subsequent political battles.

Reagan and his fiancée, the movie actress Jane Wyman, apply for a marriage license in Los Angeles on January 20, 1940. Having met in 1938 during the filming of *Brother Rat*, in which each of them had minor roles, Reagan and Wyman were married on January 26 in Glendale, California.

On January 4, 1941 — Wyman's 27th birthday — the Reagans' daughter Maureen was born. But during the building of a new eight-room house on a hill overlooking Hollywood, the first signs of strain in the marriage appeared. Reagan was now earning an impressive $1,000 a week but would not allow Wyman to buy new furniture. She was accustomed to purchasing whatever she wanted whether she had the money or not, but Reagan refused to go into debt. In those days Reagan believed debt financing a very bad business.

Also in 1941, Reagan played the role he would always consider his best, that of the playboy Drake McHugh, in the steamy small-town saga *King's Row*. In the best-known scene in the film, the philandering McHugh realizes that his legs have been unnecessarily amputated. Waking from the operation, he cries out, "Where's the rest of me?" Almost a quarter of a century later, that line became the title of Reagan's autobiography.

Reagan expected this role to advance him to the ranks of Hollywood's biggest stars, but it looked as if this would not happen. By the time the film was

Ann Sheridan, Ronald Reagan, and Robert Cummings (left to right) film a scene from *King's Row*, a 1941 melodrama set in small-town America. Movie critic James Agate called *King's Row* "half masterpiece and half junk." Most critics, however, praised Reagan's performance.

released in 1942, the United States had entered World War II, and Reagan, a member of the army reserve, had been called to active duty. But Reagan was disqualified from combat because of his near-sightedness. Instead he did a brief stint at Fort Mason in San Francisco before being transferred to the First Motion Picture Unit of the Army Air Corps, which operated out of the old Hal Roach studios, a few miles from Warner Brothers. Reagan spent the remainder of the war years working at the studio affectionately known as "Fort Roach" and never saw active duty.

For the most part, Reagan was featured in pilot-training films, which was ironic because Reagan himself refused to fly. The only Hollywood film he made during the war was *This Is the Army*, a musical by Irving Berlin — composer of "God Bless America." In order to act in the film, Reagan was temporarily detached from his unit.

Yet, as far as America was concerned, Reagan was an active combatant in the fighting overseas. This false image was propagated by the press, which ran stories about Wyman bravely seeing her husband off to war. In an interview, Reagan said he looked forward to the war's end, when he could return home and sleep beside his wife again. This was a puzzling statement because Reagan spent every night of the war at home. The "war-torn" Reagans adopted a son, Michael, in March 1945, nine months before Reagan's discharge from the army. In 1946, Reagan was welcomed back to Hollywood as a hero. But the Hollywood to which he "returned" was quite different from the one he had "left."

For years, Reagan had refused membership in the Screen Actors Guild (SAG) until a friend talked him into joining in 1938. Three years later, he became a member of the board of directors. When he "returned" from the war, Reagan was made guild president, after Robert Montgomery, an actor turned producer, resigned to avoid a conflict of interest. The year was 1946, and a jurisdictional dispute between rival stagehand unions had caused a strike. Reagan moved quickly to end it, convinced that the strike was part of a Communist plot.

> *My education was completed when I walked into the board room. I saw it was crammed with the famous men of the business. I knew then that I was beginning to find the rest of me.*
> —RONALD REAGAN
> on joining the board of directors of the Screen Actors Guild

Jane Wyman and one-year-old Maureen Elizabeth say good-bye to their husband and father, Lieutenant Ronald Reagan, as he leaves to report for military service in San Francisco. Disqualified from serving active duty because of poor eyesight, Reagan spent the World War II years making training films for the army at the Hal Roach studios in Hollywood.

Socialist ideas had become common currency in American intellectual circles in the 1930s and may have influenced aspects of President Roosevelt's New Deal, an elaborate plan to lift America out of economic depression through government-sponsored employment programs. But the notion of centralized planning was inimical to a nation founded on self-determination. During World War II, the United States — the world's leading capitalist country — and the Soviet Union — the world's leading Communist power — were allied in the fight against Nazi Germany. But after the Nazis were vanquished in 1945, the victors resumed a steady march toward a confrontation with each other. Europe had been carved into Russian and American spheres of influence, and each superpower sought dominance in the Third World. But because both sides possessed life-threatening nuclear weapons, they could not battle openly. In the ensuing cold war, Communists and alleged Communists were hounded in the United States, and in Hollywood there ensued a shameless witch-hunt.

Historians refer to the time before the invention of television as the golden age of Hollywood. It was a time when moviegoing was a way of life for Americans. The silver screen provided black-and-white images of the past and present, documenting America's longings and ideals. In the battle for the hearts and minds of Americans, movies were a powerful tool that no longer seemed safe in the hands of those Americans who had been influenced — particularly during the depression — by Communist ideology, which was founded on the principle "from each according to his abilities, to each according to his needs." Reagan was not immune to such concepts and would later refer to his earlier self as "a near-hopeless hemophiliac liberal." But by 1946, when he was 35, Reagan had become a staunch anti-Communist.

His brother Neil — by then a major player in Hollywood advertising — had long been a vocal anti-Communist, but Ronald Reagan was not convinced that there was a dangerous Communist threat lurking in America until July 1946. That year he helped draft a resolution affirming SAG's commitment to free enterprise and repudiating communism in America. Reagan brought it before the Hollywood Independent Citizens Committee of the Arts, Sciences, and Professions, but the resolution never came to a vote. It was blocked by influential committee members who either disagreed with the position of the resolution or who felt SAG should refrain from taking any position at all. Reagan saw the defeat as orchestrated by Communists. Outraged, he resigned from the board of directors and began to speak out fervently against what he perceived as the Communist menace in America.

Neil Reagan was recruited as a spy for the Federal Bureau of Investigation (FBI), and on April 10, 1947, Ronald Reagan — together with Jane Wyman — named at least six suspected Communists in a secret meeting with FBI agents. This information was considered so valuable that agents continued to meet with Reagan — three times in 1947 alone — and issued him an informant's code number, T-10.

It's true the Senator used a shotgun when a rifle was needed, injuring the innocent along with the guilty. Nevertheless, his broadsides should not be used today to infer that all who opposed Communist subversion were hysterical zealots.
—RONALD REAGAN
in 1979, on
Joseph McCarthy,
chairman of the House Un-American Activities
Committee

On October 23, 1947, Reagan, as head of the Screen Actors Guild, testifies before the House Un-American Activities Committee during its investigation of alleged Communist infiltration of the motion picture industry. Such inquiries into alleged Communist activities were part of a "red scare" that ruined the careers of many Americans during the 1940s and 1950s.

On October 23, 1947, Reagan testified before the House Un-American Activities Committee. Though he did not name names, as he had for the FBI, Reagan made clear his concern about the Communist threat to America.

In November 1947, SAG elected Reagan to the first of what would eventually be five consecutive terms he would serve as guild president. As president he supported a resolution aimed at keeping Communists and Communist sympathizers from holding important positions in SAG. The resolution required anyone seeking such a position to sign an affidavit denying past or present membership in the Communist party.

During the subsequent years in which numerous writers, directors, and actors were barred from Hollywood in a process known as blacklisting, Reagan insisted that no blacklist existed. He maintained that those individuals exiled from the industry were being denied work because they had espoused ideas that were unpopular with producers, who had simply decided not to hire them. Thus, Reagan exhibted an early talent for spin doctoring.

In 1948, Reagan cofounded the Labor League of Hollywood Voters to check the anti-Communist credentials of political candidates. The following year, he became cofounder and vice-president of the Motion Picture Industrial Council, a public relations committee designed to convince the public that Hollywood was free of Communist influence. He also sat on the SAG committee for clearing members of the film community charged with Communist ties.

Meanwhile, Reagan's marriage fell apart. While his career languished, Wyman's skyrocketed during the war because of her fine performances in *The Lost Weekend* and *The Yearling*. During 1947, when Wyman was pregnant again, Reagan contracted viral pneumonia. He was in the hospital recovering from this illness and was thus unable to be with his wife when she gave birth to a premature baby girl. The infant died the next day. After her baby's death, Wyman threw herself into the role of a deaf-mute in *Johnny Belinda*. Her performance won her the Oscar for best actress in 1948, and by the time she was awarded the prestigious prize, the Reagans had separated. Their divorce was granted on June 28, 1949, and made final on July 18. Wyman was awarded custody of the children.

Reagan took a somewhat sardonic view of the breakup. While lecturing on the film industry's behalf soon after, Reagan surprised audiences by joking sarcastically about the high success rate of Hollywood marriages.

Reagan was less sanguine about his "marriage" to Warner Brothers. Lew Wasserman — of Reagan's talent agency, MCA — had negotiated a seven-year, million-dollar contract for Reagan, but Reagan began complaining about "lightweight" roles and was particularly upset about never being cast in cowboy movies. In 1950, Wasserman renegotiated, committing Reagan to a single picture a year, and got him a five-year, five-picture deal with Universal Studios. Essentially, Reagan had become a free-lance actor, able to choose his own roles.

Reagan's first western was delayed until 1951 because while playing baseball he had slid into first base and broken his right thigh in six places. Eventually, he made three more westerns. Also in 1951, Reagan costarred with a chimpanzee in *Bedtime for Bonzo*. Reagan gave an acceptable performance but never lived down being upstaged by a chimpanzee.

That same year, Reagan met Nancy Davis, a minor movie actress who was worried about the way her name kept showing up on Communist mailing lists. She sought to clear her name by appealing to the president of SAG, although the president's intervention was not strictly necessary.

Born in 1921 to Edith Luckett, a well-known stage actress, and a father who left home within a year of her birth, Nancy lived with relatives until Luckett left the stage to marry Loyal Davis, a successful Chicago neurosurgeon, who adopted the young girl and gave her his last name. The Davises remained friendly with theater people, and when Nancy graduated from Smith College in 1943, family connections helped her career on the stage — Zasu Pitts, an American star of stage and screen, put her in a road show, and Mary Martin, another major Ameri-

In the 1953 movie *Law and Order*, Reagan played a cowboy-turned-marshall bent on cleaning up Cottonwood, a fictitious frontier town victimized by violence and corruption. The film was a sequel to a 1932 movie by the same name starring Walter Huston.

Soon after his divorce from Jane Wyman in June 1949, Ronald Reagan met the MGM actress Nancy Davis, and the two were married on March 4, 1952. Their first child, Patricia Ann, was born less than eight months later, on October 22.

can actress, got her a part on Broadway. Not every aspiring young actress got to date film heartthrob Clark Gable, but thanks to her connections Nancy Davis did. Soon she went to Hollywood, where she told studio publicists that her greatest ambition was to have a happy marriage. This wish began to come true when she married Ronald Reagan on March 4, 1952.

After spending their honeymoon in Arizona, the Reagans lived in Nancy's apartment until they bought a small house in Pacific Palisades, California. Nancy gave birth to a daughter, Patricia, on October 22, 1952. By then, Reagan had sold an 8-acre ranch acquired during his first marriage and purchased two parcels of land comprising some 300 acres in the hills of Santa Monica, north of Los Angeles. The $85,000 property abutted 2,500 acres owned by the 20th Century Fox film studios.

That year, SAG president Reagan also signed a waiver that benefited his agency, MCA. At that time, talent agencies were barred from producing because allowing them to do so created the potential for conflicts of interest. MCA, however, wanted to produce for television. (Reagan had acted on television as early as December 7, 1950, starring in an episode of "Airflyte Theatre," despite his fears that television would destroy the movie industry.) In signing the waiver allowing MCA to become the only agency to produce, Reagan claimed he had won a victory for actors because MCA agreed to grant them residuals —additional fees when programs were rebroadcast.

With his film career stalled, Reagan worked in a Las Vegas nightclub. Because he did not sing or dance and was not a comedian, he served as a genial emcee, and he might have continued in that role if he had not so disliked the late hours and dissolute life of the gambling town.

In 1954, MCA was granted an extension of its 1952 production waiver 24 hours before SAG formally extended the ban preventing other agencies

With his movie career sputtering, Reagan performs as a singing waiter at the Last Frontier Hotel in Las Vegas, Nevada, in 1954. His brief period of hard luck took a turn for the better later that year, when he signed a contract to host a new television show sponsored by General Electric.

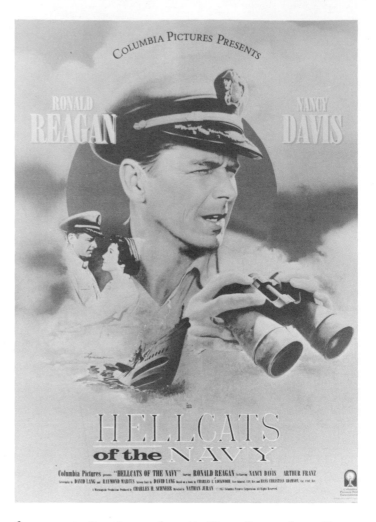

In the jingoistic potboiler *Hellcats of the Navy*, Ronald Reagan played the role of a daring World War II submarine commander in the South Pacific. The movie — which costarred his wife, Nancy — premiered in 1957 and marked Ronald Reagan's 52nd film appearance.

from engaging in such activities. Coincidentally or not, MCA produced "General Electric Theater" and signed SAG board member Reagan as host and occasional star of the new television series. (It may also have been coincidental that Nancy Davis, also on the board, would play the female lead in four episodes of "General Electric Theater." In fact, four of the six actors on SAG's board acted for the program.) Reagan's contract called for a $125,000 annual payment, which was soon increased to $150,000. General Electric's generosity to the Reagans extended to turning the Reagans' Pacific Palisades home into a showplace — the "House of the Future" — by installing every imaginable electrical convenience.

Busy with television, Reagan made only one movie in 1955. His last feature film, *Hellcats of the Navy* —costarring his wife—premiered on April 11, 1957. It was Reagan's 52nd film appearance.

By the time their son Ronald Prescott was born to the Reagans on May 28, 1958, "General Electric Theater" was their sole source of income. In 1959, Reagan sought a portion of the show's earnings from reruns, and MCA's producing entity, MCA Revue Productions, made him a coproducer, with rights to 25 percent of the program's proceeds.

That same year, Reagan returned to the SAG presidency in time to settle another dispute. Television had grown into a major industry, constantly in need of new "product." The tremendous number of preexisting movies could constitute a good part of that product, but actors wanted residuals for each time their movies were shown on television.

MCA had purchased 700 films from Paramount Studios for television release and was anxious to exploit its investment. Reagan, as SAG president, cut a deal with MCA — before the other studios settled — in which MCA would be absolved of residuals for films made prior to 1960 in exchange for a $2 million contribution to a SAG actors' fund. This contribution represented a very small fraction of the money MCA would make with its films.

Shortly after signing this deal, Reagan resigned his presidency because of a "conflict of interest," claiming that he was now a producer. But Reagan was a producer before making the deal with MCA; in fact, Reagan had first been credited as coproducer of an episode of "General Electric Theater" in 1955. Why was there no conflict of interest then?

This question was raised by the Justice Department during an investigation of MCA activities in 1962. MCA had become the dominant force in American television, responsible by 1961 for more than 40 percent of prime-time programming. The Justice Department had launched eight investigations of MCA before 1962 but had had tremendous difficulty in obtaining evidence or witnesses because everyone in Hollywood was fearful of reprisals from the powerful agency.

In testimony about the waiver granted in 1952, Reagan's photographic memory failed him. He could not remember anything that had happened in the summer of 1952, he said, because he was on an "extended honeymoon." Then he claimed he had not

A beaming Ronald and Nancy Reagan pose for an informal family portrait with their children, five-year-old Patti and one-month-old Ronald Prescott, in June 1958. By that time, Ronald Reagan had become a successful spokesman for General Electric, giving speeches throughout the country — good training for a career in politics.

participated in waiver discussions because he had spent that summer in Glacier National Park making a cowboy movie — but *Cattle Queen of Montana* was made in 1954. Pressed further by investigators, Reagan finally remembered he had avoided waiver talks because he was an MCA client.

The Justice Department seriously considered indictments against Reagan and MCA. In the end, no suits were brought against either of them because MCA divested itself of its agency, continuing as a producing outfit only.

By this time, "General Electric Theater" was coming to the end of its long run, but another aspect of Reagan's General Electric contract had already prepared him for a change of careers.

As part of his television deal, Reagan toured the country ten weeks a year, promoting G.E. products. General Electric had 139 plants in 38 states, and between 1954 and 1962, Reagan visited each one, meeting all 250,000 employees. In one factory, Reagan signed 10,000 photographs in 2 days. In the Louisville, Kentucky, plant, he walked the entire length of the 46-mile assembly line twice, and his feet became so swollen that he had to remove his shoelaces to do it.

During these appearances, Reagan developed a speech in which he espoused conservative political ideas and made appealing and often comical self-deprecatory statements. His folksy anecdotes were culled mainly from newspaper and magazine clippings. General Electric gave Reagan the freedom to say whatever he wanted during his engagements until the Tennessee Valley Authority threatened to cancel contracts worth $50 million because of a derogatory paragraph in the speech. Even though General Electric was willing to stand behind its spokesman, Reagan was flexible: He dropped the paragraph.

Reagan found that making speeches could be a profitable sideline and began speaking at other gatherings. As a spokesman for a large corporation, Reagan was playing a role he was quite comfortable playing and one he would play throughout his political career.

We drove him to the utmost limits. We saturated him in Middle America.
—EDWARD LANGLEY of General Electric, on Reagan's years as GE spokesman

4

Mr. Reagan Goes to Sacramento

As late as 1950, Reagan still supported the Democratic party, including Helen Gahagan Douglas, who lost a Senate seat to Republican Richard Nixon when smeared as a Communist. Even in 1952, Reagan evinced devotion to the Democrats in a telegram to Dwight Eisenhower — the World War II hero sought as presidential candidate by both major parties — urging him to accept the Democratic nomination. But clearly Reagan was becoming more conservative. His father-in-law — a vociferous conservative — may have aided in the transformation, but the root of it was simple: Reagan was becoming a wealthy man.

At the peak of his movie career, Reagan earned $3,500 a week, placing him in the highest federal tax bracket, which at that time took as much as 90 percent of one's income. To many, the tax laws seemed unfair and antiproductive. In the film industry, highly paid actors such as Reagan — who had formerly made eight pictures a year — restricted

I don't know, I've never played a governor.
—RONALD REAGAN in 1966, after being asked what kind of governor he would be

An ecstatic San Francisco crowd greets California gubernatorial candidate Ronald Reagan with a shower of ticker tape in November 1966. By the time Reagan ran for governor of California, many considered the former Democrat a right-wing extremist.

themselves to four because taxes made more work almost worthless. Reagan sought general tax reform but believed actors particularly deserved a tax break. He maintained that actors should be permitted a personal depreciation allowance because their productive years might be limited to youth.

By 1960, Reagan was a well-known conservative spokesman, and Republican officials asked him to campaign for Nixon's bid for the presidency. Reagan offered to reregister as a Republican but — told he would be more valuable as a renegade — remained a Democrat in name only.

At the end of eight years on "General Electric Theater," Reagan's political views began to dominate the speeches he gave, and General Electric asked him to refrain from political commentary and confine himself to selling G.E. products. Reagan refused, and General Electric canceled the show. (Another factor, no doubt, was that "Bonanza," a western series, had pulled ahead in the ratings.) That same year, 1962, Reagan became a Republican. Also that year, he became the host and occasional actor on another television series, "Death Valley Days," sponsored by Boraxo — a company for which his brother, Neil, was an advertising executive. MCA acted as Reagan's agent in the deal. The "Death Valley Days" job continued until 1964, when Reagan made his final acting appearance in a made-for-television movie produced by MCA. *The Killers*, too violent for television in those days, was released theatrically. It was the only movie in which Reagan played a villain, and he later regretted taking on the role.

Politics now became Reagan's primary interest. On October 27, 1964, he made a television speech for Republican presidential candidate Barry Goldwater — an ultraconservative whose shoot-from-the-lip attacks on the Soviet Union made many Americans fearful that a Goldwater presidency would lead to war. "A Time for Choosing" — as Reagan's Goldwater speech was called — is generally considered the start of his political career.

The California millionaire Holmes P. Tuttle, who had previously heard Reagan speak and befriended

Ultraconservative Barry Goldwater makes a bid for the presidency during the 1964 California Republican primary. Reagan's speech in support of Goldwater — a high point in an otherwise disastrous campaign — marked Reagan's entrance into politics.

him, helped finance the broadcast. Goldwater suffered ignominious defeat, but Reagan's speech raised $1 million for Republican candidates. Tuttle and several millionaire friends decided to run Reagan for governor of California in 1966.

Reagan had already shown interest in a political career by writing an autobiography (*Where's the Rest of Me?*, published in 1965). As early as 1962 he had exchanged letters with daughter Maureen on the subject of entering politics. She had urged him to become California's governor, but he had insisted it would be better to become president.

Tuttle and his friends hired the political management firm of Stuart Spencer and Bill Roberts to organize Reagan's campaign. After seeing the ultra-conservative Goldwater go down in flames, Spencer and Roberts hoped Reagan was not the right-wing extremist he seemed to be. In a series of personal meetings with Spencer and Roberts, Reagan was able to calm their fears.

Roberts and Tuttle created an organization called the Friends of Ronald Reagan, which — supported by 41 wealthy donors — sent a fundraising letter to Republican activists late in the spring of 1965. The campaign raised money and garnered enthusiastic support for the Republicans.

Spencer and Roberts found Reagan to be bright but soon realized that he was seriously uninformed on important issues and had a bad habit of making statements that simply were not true. They contracted the Behavior Science Corporation (BASICO) to remake their candidate through behavior modification techniques.

After interviewing Reagan and analyzing his speeches, BASICO focused on 17 issues, creating 8 black books of facts with which Reagan would make his points. The facts were transferred to five-by-eight-inch index cards, and for six months someone from BASICO accompanied Reagan to every campaign stop. When confronted with difficult questions, Reagan consulted the men from BASICO before answering.

California voters were unhappy with incumbent

governor Edmund Brown. The growing costs of state and local government seemed to exceed delivered services, and little was being done to soothe deepening class, racial, and generational conflicts. For example, in the fall of 1964, when political rallies were prohibited outside the University of California at Berkeley, Mario Savio began the Free Speech Movement. On December 3, some 700 students seized control of the administration building, and although Brown would eventually heed law officers' advice and break the movement with mass arrests, he was criticized for not acting quickly. Continuing unrest was also held against him. Similarly, Brown was held responsible for riots in Watts, a Los Angeles ghetto, in 1965, at a time when Brown was vacationing in Greece. In March 1966, when riots in Watts erupted again, voters were reminded of Brown's absence the year before.

Though these troubles, like the increase in the use of drugs on college campuses and violent clashes over America's involvement in Vietnam, reflected nationwide problems and could not fairly be blamed on Brown, voters are not necessarily fair. Moreover, Brown helped defeat himself by failing to take the Reagan challenge seriously. He considered Reagan an actor, not a politician.

The Spencer-Roberts team proved Brown wrong, or at least proved that an actor could be a fine politician. Guided by public opinion polls, they had Reagan focus on Brown's "failed leadership," the "university mess," high taxes, and the rising cost of welfare. In speech after speech, Reagan condemned student dissidents, apparently changing his position since participating himself in a student strike while he was at Eureka College. Reagan was his handlers' dream candidate. As in Hollywood, he took direction well and mostly stuck to the script. He had pat answers for most questions but was a good enough actor to deliver them each time as if he had just thought them up.

Still, he did not always walk without stumbling. At the National Negro Republican Assembly on March 6, 1966, for example, pressed on his oppo-

For many years now, you and I have been shushed like children and told there are no simple answers to complex problems which are beyond comprehension. Well, the truth is, there are simple answers— there just are not easy ones.
—RONALD REAGAN
as governor of California

Some 8,000 demonstrators take to the streets of Berkeley, California, in the 1960s to protest U.S. military intervention in Southeast Asia. In his campaign rhetoric, Reagan blamed California governor Edmund Brown for the social unrest that was sweeping the state. Reagan beat the incumbent in a landslide victory.

sition to the federal Civil Rights Act of 1964, Reagan lashed out at those who would accuse him of racism and stormed out of the auditorium. Once he was persuaded to return, Reagan explained his objection to the Civil Rights Act on constitutional grounds.

The episode caused minimal damage but taught Reagan's handlers an important lesson. He had lost his temper primarily because he was tired. From then on, afternoon naps were scheduled, and the remainder of the campaign went smoothly: There were no blowups, and nobody seemed to notice that candidate Reagan articulated general goals but no specific programs. Ultimately, Reagan defeated Brown by nearly a million votes. The governor-elect's reaction to this landslide victory was, "My God, what do we do now?"

That was a good question because neither Reagan nor his staff understood how to run a government. Remaining in southern California, rather than going to Sacramento, the state capital, the new governor and his staff made a slow and unsteady transition. Once in Sacramento, responsibility for the transition fell to campaign manager Philip Battaglia, now Reagan's executive secretary. Battaglia had gained tremendous influence during the last month of the campaign and now regularly passed to Reagan notes on three-by-five-inch cards from which he dutifully read to the press.

At first, Reagan's millionaire backers had exercised a great deal of influence, but they lost interest when the transition moved to Sacramento. Then, Press Secretary Lyn Nofziger assumed more power, and Alameda County deputy district attorney Edwin Meese — brought in as legal affairs secretary because of his hard-line law-and-order approach to the Berkeley troubles — became Reagan's chief adviser by championing capital punishment, which Reagan supported.

On January 1, 1967, at one minute past midnight, Reagan became governor of California. (Actually, the oath of office had been scheduled for 10 minutes past midnight but was moved up on advice from Mrs. Reagan's astrologer.) The inaugural celebration was elaborate and costly, designed by the Walt Disney Studios.

Taft Schreiber, MCA's "Republican donor," negotiated the sale of most of Reagan's Santa Monica land to 20th Century Fox for nearly $2 million, a deal consummated on January 31, 1967. Reagan used his remaining 54-acre parcel as a down payment on a 778-acre ranch in Riverside County. Profits from his land deals went into tax shelters. For the next 4 years Reagan would pay as little as $1,000 a year in state taxes.

The state's finances were not as good as Reagan's. Although California's constitution required a balanced budget, Governor Brown had got around the law (and avoided a tax increase in an election year)

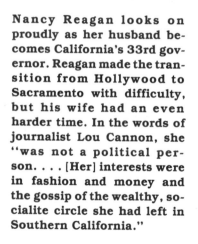

Nancy Reagan looks on proudly as her husband becomes California's 33rd governor. Reagan made the transition from Hollywood to Sacramento with difficulty, but his wife had an even harder time. In the words of journalist Lou Cannon, she "was not a political person. . . . [Her] interests were in fashion and money and the gossip of the wealthy, socialite circle she had left in Southern California."

by switching the state's accounting from a cash to an accrual basis. This meant that the state could count revenues as they came due rather than as they were collected.

Unfortunately, the change was not properly funded, and Reagan faced an immediate deficit debacle. After several candidates for state finance director turned down the job, Gordon Paul Smith, a management consultant, was hired. With only 2 weeks to prepare the massive state budget, Smith proposed a 10 percent across-the-board budget cut. Reagan loved this simple idea, but it did not take into account the way the government functioned. Some ill-managed programs could accommodate cuts, but well-run programs suffered.

A state hiring freeze was instituted, and state employees were asked to work voluntarily on the Lincoln's Birthday and Washington's Birthday holidays (less than two percent did). A freeze was imposed on automobile purchases, out-of-state travel was drastically curtailed, plans for a new state office building were shelved, and the state airplane was sold. The motor vehicle freeze was particularly ill conceived: Some 40 trucks had been purchased without the trailers needed to make them useful.

Reagan presented these proposals in a televised speech that convinced the voters, but reality was less forgiving than the electorate. For example, recommended cuts in mental hospital funds — made possible by powerful tranquilizers that allowed patients to be released into community treatment programs, reducing the hospital population by almost 60 percent — failed to recognize ongoing plant-maintenance costs or the remaining patients, who constituted the most difficult cases. Reagan refused to visit a facility or to review a memo stating that the hospitals had been severely understaffed since 1952.

As the negative effect of the budget cuts was felt, Reagan relented, and budgets were restored. The resulting fiscal shortfall could not be made up by such minor revenue boosters as increased tuition at the University of California. Reluctantly, tax-hating Reagan raised state income taxes.

He was also reluctant to increase state welfare payments, but the federal government threatened to cut off aid unless he did. A new welfare reform bill — a bipartisan effort for which Reagan took credit — reduced the state's welfare rolls significantly, though not much more than could be accounted for by slowed population growth.

Reagan's pet project was the Community Work Experience Program, touted as a model for welfare reform nationwide. But a pilot program for 30,000 participants failed because most welfare recipients either lacked the skills to become useful employees or were mothers of dependent children. Only 9,600 were assigned jobs before the program was abolished in 1975.

Meanwhile, Reagan was straying from the script and getting himself into trouble. For example, on February 20, 1967, Reagan claimed that no American had ever been denied medical treatment due to lack of funds, even when many Americans lacked basic health care insurance. Again, on March 15, discussing the fate of the Redwood National Park, Reagan lapsed when he insisted there was nothing particularly beautiful about that particular stand of trees, except that they were a little higher than the others.

Reagan was not heavily burdened with the chores of government. Unlike his predecessors, he left his office by 5:00 P.M. daily, to go home for dinner and television viewing. His favorite program was "Mis-

Reagan looks up from his desk during his first day on the job as California governor. In his campaign rhetoric, Governor Reagan, a staunch conservative, promised "to squeeze, cut, and trim" the cost of government.

sion Impossible." Still, Mrs. Reagan tried to reduce pressures on her husband and make sure he got plenty of rest. She was assisted by staffer Michael Deaver, who became unusually close to the Reagans, in part because he played the piano — Mrs. Reagan loved a good sing-along.

Amenable to his wife's idea that he do less work himself and delegate more responsibility, Reagan let others handle much of the governing of California. But this hands-off approach soon created problems, some of them embarrassing. One such problem involved rumors of homosexual activity among Reagan's staff. Meese and Nofziger investigated the matter without informing Reagan, and when the rumors proved true, they kept him in the dark as long as possible. When he was told, Reagan was shocked by the news and demanded resignations from the individuals named, promising to make no comment if they resigned promptly. Nevertheless, the press found out and pressured the governor for a statement, which he refused to make. When the story would not go away, Nofziger finally confirmed it, but without telling Reagan he had done so. Confronted by the press again, Reagan denied the entire affair. Even when the botched cover-up was revealed, Reagan insisted he had done right in attempting to protect the reputations of the accused.

Despite Reagan's mixed first-year record, his backers pushed him to seek the Republican nomination for president in 1968, in opposition to the more moderate front-runner, Nixon. Despite doubts, Reagan agreed to run, and — although he was not a declared candidate but only a favorite son from California — he hit the campaign trail. While touring the country, he refused to speak out in the South against Alabama governor George Wallace's segregationist policies — again casting doubt on his civil rights stance.

Despite Nixon's delegate lead, Reagan declared his candidacy at the nominating convention. During the campaign, Nixon's support was purportedly soft in the South, but as the primary season progressed, the southern delegations strongly supported Nixon. Consequently, Reagan's last-minute grab for the

> *We've got to recognize that where the preservation of a natural resource like the redwoods is concerned, that there is a common sense limit. I mean, if you've looked at a hundred thousand acres or so of trees, you know, a tree is a tree, how many more do you need to look at?*
> —RONALD REAGAN
> in a speech on environmental issues as governor of California

nomination was embarrassing, but his abortive candidacy had aroused fervor and laid the groundwork for future efforts.

Back in California, student antiwar demonstrations grew increasingly unruly. Some supported U.S. involvement in Vietnam, believing that "democratic" South Vietnam's effort to defeat Communist North Vietnam was a cause worth fighting for, whereas many others viewed American involvement in Southeast Asia as imperialist or at best futile. Violent antiwar demonstrations took place on campuses and on the streets. On February 5, 1969, Reagan declared a state of emergency and sent the state's highway patrol to protect the Berkeley campus from "criminal anarchists" and "off-campus revolutionaries." In May, student protesters occupied land owned by the university, called it "People's Park," and stoned police who tried to evict them.

Enthusiastic supporters of Ronald Reagan for president carry signs under a cluster of festive balloons at the Republican National Convention in Miami, Florida, in 1968. Reagan's bid for the Republican presidential nomination that year was ill advised, poorly planned, and finally a debacle.

On May 15, the protest became a bloody riot: Marchers threw tear-gas canisters back at the police, who opened fire; a 25-year-old student was killed by gunfire; scores were injured; hundreds were arrested. When the outnumbered lawmen could no longer guarantee citizen safety, Reagan called out the National Guard. Unofficially, Berkeley was ruled by martial law for 17 days.

To many desirous of societal change, Reagan now embodied the reactionary old guard. To many more, Reagan was a hero, and his stern actions helped him get reelected in 1970. His Democratic challenger — Jesse Unruh, leader of the state assembly — campaigned ineffectively. Reagan refused to debate him, outspent him substantially, and won by a narrow margin.

Reagan's second gubernatorial term was significantly less divisive than his first. He became more adept at political arts, particularly compromise, and forged an excellent working relationship with the state assembly's new leader, Bob Moretti. Although he had long resisted a state withholding tax, he accepted it in 1971. In 1972, he used federal revenue sharing, the surplus generated by the 1967 tax increase, and a 1-cent increase in the state sales tax to provide $1 billion in property tax relief and enhance local school budgets.

The biggest disappointment of Reagan's second term was the 1973 failure of Proposition One, designed to limit government spending. In a regrettable off-the-cuff remark, Reagan helped defeat the proposition himself by acknowledging that even though voters did not understand the language of the proposal, that did not matter because he did not understand it either.

Reagan left the governor's office at the end of 1974. His advisers had urged him to seek a third term, but he had supported a constitutional amendment limiting service to two terms and had pledged to limit himself when the amendment was rejected.

Before Reagan left office, the California State Parks and Recreation Department purchased a large parcel of land owned by 20th Century Fox, including the property the studios had bought from

Reagan at the beginning of his term of office. In December 1974, Reagan sold his acreage in Riverside County to a trust headed by Jules Stein (the "Democratic donor" at MCA) for $856,000. For $527,000, he bought a 667-acre ranch in Santa Barbara that he called Rancho del Cielo. He took advantage of an "agricultural preserve" provision to lower his taxes on Rancho del Cielo by raising 22 head of cattle. The savings gained by this maneuver amounted to more than $41,000 in 1979 alone. Private life had its appeal.

Governor Reagan chats with students on the University of California campus in Los Angeles. Reagan, who was re-elected governor in 1970, had vowed to reduce the cost of government, but during his 2 terms the state's annual budget increased from $4.6 billion to $10.2 billion.

5

A Role Worth Fighting For

In 1974, crooner Pat Boone, wearing his customary white buckskin shoes and winning smile, brought Reverend George Otis and several friends to visit Governor and Mrs. Reagan in Sacramento. Before leaving, the group joined hands in a prayer circle, and Reverend Otis, holding Reagan's hand, felt a pulsing in his arm, a shaking he could not stop. The reverend believed himself possessed by the Holy Spirit and without volition changed the words of his prayer: "My son, if you walk uprightly before me, you will reside at 1600 Pennsylvania Avenue." The person holding Reagan's other hand felt a "bolt of electricity" shoot up his arm. Reagan, too, felt the presidency was his calling. But first he had to make money.

> *Now, I hope and pray that this administration is successful. And that would take care of '76. Because it's never—in my book—it's never been important who's in the White House, it's what's done.*
>
> —RONALD REAGAN
> referring to the Ford administration while alluding to his own 1976 candidacy

The White House, Washington, D.C. When Reagan decided to seek the Republican nomination for president in 1976, the party was grossly unpopular with the American people. Many believed — following the revelations of the Watergate scandal — that Republican president Richard Nixon, who resigned in 1974, had betrayed their trust and disgraced the presidency.

Presidential candidate Reagan campaigns in New Hampshire in January 1976. Despite the Republican party's post-Watergate malaise and low status among voters, Reagan was as popular as ever on the campaign trail, and though he lost the nomination to Gerald Ford, Reagan was poised for a 1980 bid.

As a political commentator, Reagan had a column appearing in 174 newspapers, and his views were aired on more than 200 radio stations. In 1975 alone he earned as much as $800,000. Because the law required equal time on the airwaves for political opponents, Reagan delayed announcing his 1976 candidacy as long as possible, which did not prevent him from campaigning as an undeclared candidate.

In 1975, the Republican Gerald R. Ford sat in the White House, having assumed the presidency in August 1974 after Richard Nixon resigned — the first president in history to do so — in the wake of the Watergate scandal.

Reagan had been a staunch supporter of Nixon.
Even as others deserted Nixon, Reagan stood by
him. Even after Nixon resigned in shame, Reagan
believed he and his associates had done no wrong
in burglarizing Democratic headquarters during
the 1972 campaign and covering up the scandal by
lying to Congress and destroying evidence. To Reagan, these men had not been criminals "at heart."

It is hard to understand what Reagan admired in
Nixon. Reagan opposed Nixon's pursuit of détente
with the Russians (détente — a French word for re-
laxation of tensions — entailed cultural and economic exchanges, including the sale of large

quantities of U.S. grain to the agriculturally back-ward Soviet Union), the SALT negotiations (Strategic Arms Limitation Talks, which had resulted in the signing of SALT I by President Nixon and Soviet leader Leonid Brezhnev on May 26, 1972, during a dramatic visit to Moscow by Nixon), and the diplomatic recognition of the Communist People's Republic of China. (The Nationalist government of "democratic" Taiwan had been recognized by the United States as the legitimate government of China since the People's Republic was established in 1949.) Nevertheless, Nixon was a president to Reagan's liking, and Ford was not.

Reagan objected to Ford's continuing pursuit of détente — which Reagan believed was a policy designed to make America second best — to ongoing SALT negotiations, to Ford's signing of the Panama Canal treaties (negotiated since the mid-1960s in an attempt to turn over the Panama Canal Zone and the canal itself to the people of Panama), and to Ford's selection of the moderate Republican Nelson Rockefeller as his vice-president. (Bowing to conservative pressure, Ford "allowed" Rockefeller to remove himself from the ticket for 1976.) Reagan also objected strongly to Ford's program of amnesty for Vietnam war–era draft dodgers, and blamed the $52 billion federal deficit on Ford. To Reagan, Ford was a weak president and a weak candidate, a "caretaker," not a leader.

Ford was the president, and it is difficult — and politically dangerous — to try to unseat a president from one's own party. For this reason, Reagan briefly considered running for president as a third-party candidate. When his old friend Tuttle insisted that he was a Republican and should remain one, Reagan decided to challenge Ford for the nomination.

While campaigning in 1975, Reagan made several self-damaging statements, the most bizarre of which was the story of how a black kitchen worker on a navy vessel had integrated U.S. military forces by using a machine gun against the attacking Japanese during the surprise attack on Pearl Harbor,

We're not saying that President Ford is not doing a good job; we feel he is. But Governor Reagan could do a better job, because he is totally independent of the federal government scene.

—PAUL LAXALT
U.S. senator from Nevada,
supporting the Reagan
candidacy in 1975

Hawaii, in 1941. The armed services were actually integrated by executive order by President Truman in 1948, but Reagan insisted on his story, claiming to remember the powerful if mythical scene as if he had experienced it himself. He had never even been in Hawaii.

On September 26, 1975, Reagan enunciated a bold economic proposal in a speech based on the ideas of staffer Jeffrey Bell, asserting that states should take responsibility for welfare, education, housing, food stamps, Medicare, and community and regional development, rather than the federal government. This transfer of authority, according to Reagan, would reduce federal outlays by over $90 billion, balance the budget, reduce the national debt by $5 billion, and allow for federal income tax cuts averaging 23 percent.

Unfortunately, no one on Reagan's staff had analyzed the $90 billion figure, nor could they explain exactly where the money would come from. Furthermore, such a revamping of federal policy would likely result in higher rates of unemployment, the bankruptcy of many states and cities, and a continuation of the downward trend in the recession-riddled housing and construction industries.

Reagan's best campaign issue in 1976 was the Panama Canal treaties, which provoked an emotional response, but Ford's early success in Republican primaries put Reagan on the defensive. Throughout the campaign, Reagan was forced to fend off reporters' repeated inquiries as to when he would drop out of the race. The assumption that he would drop out hurt his chances to succeed.

But Reagan was obstinate. The more he was pressed to quit, the more he insisted he would not. A surprise win in the North Carolina primary improved his position, and Reagan stayed in the running right through the convention in Kansas City, where Ford led slightly in the delegate count. The two candidates scrambled for uncommitted delegates, but Ford did not need many more to win.

In a bold, last-ditch effort recommended by campaign manager John Sears and a senior adviser,

> *I think he really believed his candidacy wouldn't be divisive, but I knew he was wrong. How can you challenge an incumbent president of your own party and not be divisive?*
> —GERALD R. FORD
> on Reagan's bid for the Republican nomination for president in 1976

Nevada senator Paul Laxalt, Reagan took the unprecedented step of preannouncing his vice-presidential candidate. Richard S. Schweiker, senator from Pennsylvania and a liberal compared to Reagan, was chosen to broaden Reagan's appeal and demonstrate Reagan's reasonableness as a politician. But Schweiker was too liberal for many conservatives, who saw his selection as an unsavory political compromise.

The final delegate count was 1,187 for Ford, 1,070 for Reagan. It was a loss for Reagan, however narrow, but when Ford was defeated in the general election by Democrat Jimmy Carter, Reagan was positioned as the Republican front-runner for 1980.

Reagan returned to Rancho del Cielo, working the ranch with a hired hand, taking long rides on Arabian and quarter horses. He also returned to his lucrative career as a political commentator and never stopped running for president. With $1 million in campaign funds left over from his late surge in the 1976 primaries, Reagan formed a political action committee, Citizens for the Republic, to support Republican candidates. He also continued making speeches — 75 in 1977 alone. In the fall of 1978, he stumped for Republican candidates, keeping his face and name before the public and accruing important political debts.

Reagan announced his candidacy formally on November 13, 1979. His campaign schedule was quite brisk at first — an attempt to dispel fears that he was too old for the job. His campaign strategy was to assume that the nomination was his, to ignore his seven Republican opponents, and to concentrate his energies on attacking President Carter.

On the campaign trail, Reagan referred proudly to his record as governor of California but could not keep from misrepresenting it. For example, he claimed that he had cut government spending, when in fact he had raised it substantially.

It was easier for Reagan to attack Carter than to make a case for himself. Carter had joined Soviet leader Brezhnev in Vienna, Austria, on June 18, 1979, to sign a SALT II agreement, which Reagan strongly opposed. His distaste for SALT II stemmed from the fact that the treaty would not reduce weapon stockpiles, only slow the rate of growth.

This was a somewhat disingenuous argument. The year before, Reagan had made the phrase "window of vulnerability" a major issue, referring to that period of time — apparently soon — in which the Soviets would possess nuclear capabilities so far superior to those of the United States that they could launch a peremptory "first strike" against the United States, knocking out all land-based American missiles and virtually assuring Soviet victory in a half-hour war. This issue proved potent, although the "window of vulnerability" did not and would not exist. (A report from the Central Intelligence Agency stated that U.S. and Soviet nuclear capabilities were "roughly equivalent," although a blue-ribbon panel, appointed specifically to override that conclusion, suggested otherwise.)

SALT II was also a somewhat spurious issue, since the treaty had never been ratified by Congress, in large measure due to the Soviet Union's invasion of Afghanistan in December 1979. Carter had retaliated with an embargo on grain sales to the Soviets and the withdrawal of American athletes from the Olympics in Moscow in 1980, but Reagan criticized the grain embargo as hurtful to American farmers and inconsequential to the Soviets.

Before taking Carter on directly, Reagan did have challengers to worry about, as he discovered to his chagrin when former CIA director George Bush won a stunning victory in the Iowa caucuses. Bush had scored well by faulting Reagan's latest economic proposals, based on the supply-side economics of Arthur Laffer and Jude Wanniski. Supply-side theory suggested that steep tax cuts would lead to increased investments that would help build the economy, resulting in a larger tax base that would more than offset revenues lost by the tax cuts.

This simple, if doubtful, concept appealed to Reagan. Despite its similarity to the discredited trickle-down theory — the idea that tax breaks for the rich would eventually "trickle down" to the less fortunate

— Reagan embraced supply-side economics with his usual fervor. Bush, on the other hand, provided a memorable phrase by referring to supply-side theory as "voodoo economics."

The Bush win in Iowa spurred Reagan's competitive spirit. Uninterested in his lesser opponents, he sought to debate Bush one-on-one in New Hampshire. Since not all candidates would be invited, the Bush and Reagan campaigns would have to cover debate expenses. When the Bush campaign refused, Reagan's people paid, setting Reagan up for the one-liner that would win him the primary.

Relenting to criticism by the excluded candidates, the Reagan campaign agreed to invite them to the debate, but did not tell Bush, hoping to catch him off guard. When Reagan strode into the debating hall with the other candidates, Bush became visibly upset. Chaos ensued, and when Reagan grabbed a microphone to explain himself, the moderator ordered the microphone shut off. Red with anger, Reagan managed to say (before the technician threw the switch), "I paid for this microphone, Mr. Green."

It did not matter that the moderator's name was Breen. Reagan had shown himself to be feisty and decisive. The voters loved it, and Reagan had little difficulty winning not only New Hampshire but the Republican nomination as well.

The most dramatic choice to be made at the sewn-up nominating convention was Reagan's vice-president. Since 1976, Reagan and Gerald Ford had patched up their differences, and for several expectant days, the notion of a dream ticket was floated: Reagan for president, Ford for vice-president. It seemed an unbeatable combination, and intensive negotiations were held to discover an arrangement whereby the former president could become vice-president with dignity.

During the convention, Ford gave an extensive television interview that helped Reagan realize that a Ford vice-presidency would raise delicate constitutional issues and seriously compromise his presidential authority. Five minutes after the interview, Reagan offered the job to Bush.

Odd as this may seem, Reagan's pollster, Richard Wirthlin, had shown that a moderate on the ticket would help Reagan win, and more than anything Reagan wanted to win. Bush was enough of a politician to swallow his earlier criticisms of Reagan. He even came around to embracing supply-side theory, denying he had ever called it voodoo economics, until later when he was shown a videotape of himself making the statement.

The campaign against Carter should have been easy. Congress had scuttled virtually every one of his ambitious programs, and he was dogged by high inflation, high unemployment, and public problems with his brother Billy (embarrassing beer-drinking

Reagan has a laugh with his lawyer, Edwin Meese (left), and his campaign manager, William Casey, in Los Angeles during the 1980 presidential campaign. Both Meese and Casey would later hold key positions in the Reagan White House.

The Reagan family celebrates Ronald Reagan's nomination for president at the Republican party's 1980 national convention in Detroit. With the nominee and his wife are (left to right) their son Ronald and daughter, Patti; their son Michael (holding their grandson Cameron) with his wife, Colleen; and Maureen, the nominee's daughter from his previous marriage.

antics and a lucrative "consultancy" with Libya, suspected of supporting international terrorism). Even a tax cut could not help Carter.

Wirthlin's polls showed that the public was sensitive to social and racial issues, so the Reagan campaign scheduled a visit to a rubble-strewn lot in New York City's poverty-ravaged South Bronx, where Carter, in 1977, had promised federally sponsored rebuilding and a job training center. Hecklers surrounded Reagan, demanding to know what he

would do to help. "I can't do a damn thing for you if I don't get elected," he finally shouted. It was a one-liner almost as important as the one in New Hampshire.

Reagan pounded away at Carter for the unpreparedness of national defense, even though Carter had overseen a massive arms buildup. He derided Carter for being oblivious to the supposed Soviet drive for world domination and — at a gathering of the Veterans of Foreign Wars — spoke of the failed,

Republican presidential candidate Reagan and President Jimmy Carter, the Democratic nominee, shake hands before their debate in Cleveland in October 1980. On election day, Carter was unable to overcome the difficulties that for 4 years had plagued his administration, and Reagan became the nation's 40th president.

unpopular effort in Vietnam as "a noble cause." Reagan managed to hurt himself, though not fatally, by promising to revive relations with Taiwan at the expense of Communist China and by suggesting that the biblical story of creation should be taught in schools as an alternative to scientific Darwinism, but it would take more than these blunders to stop Reagan.

Carter compounded his own problems by beginning his campaign in Tuscumbia, Alabama, a center of Ku Klux Klan activity. He made amends by rebuking robed members of the Klan among the crowd, but that did not stop Reagan, at the Michigan State Fair, from criticizing Carter for visiting the city he claimed had given birth to the Klan. This was another untruth, for which Reagan had to apologize.

Reagan made another odd comment at St. Joseph's College in Philadelphia, claiming that Carter's newly created Department of Education had dire plans for religious schools such as St. Joseph's. When pressed, Reagan could not explain.

Carter tried to score points by attacking Reagan's record on race relations. (Reagan had been made to look bad again during the primaries when his wife telephoned from New Hampshire — on an amplified hookup — wishing aloud that he could be there to see "all these beautiful white people.") The ploy backfired, since Carter had not supported the Civil Rights Act of 1964 either.

Behind in the polls and increasingly desperate, Carter tried to portray Reagan as a warmonger. This attack raised lingering doubts in voter's minds but hurt Carter by revealing his "mean streak." Reagan capitalized by insisting it was inconceivable that anyone would want war, calling Carter's comments "unforgivable."

Reagan now claimed that he was an environmentalist but denounced the "overkill" of the Environmental Protection Agency. He also claimed that Mount Saint Helens, a volcano in Washington State that had recently erupted, had spewed more sulfur dioxide into the atmosphere in a few months than the nation's automobiles did in 10 years; that the greatest sources of air pollution were trees and vegetation; and that air pollution had been substantially controlled. None of these assertions was even slightly acquainted with the truth.

Ever responsive to Wirthlin's polls, Reagan confronted the "gender gap" — his much weaker support among women than men, perhaps resulting from his opposition to the Equal Rights Amendment and legalized abortion — by promising to name a woman to the Supreme Court. The gesture had little impact.

In a televised debate with Carter, Reagan shone, seeming relaxed and genial, while Carter appeared stiff and nervous. Once more, a one-liner from the former actor won the voters' hearts. When Carter attacked Reagan for campaigning against Medicare — a medical program for the poor and elderly — Reagan was prepared to defend himself by pointing out that he had recently supported a proposal by the American Medical Association (not realizing that offering such support was tantamount to campaigning against Medicare), but it was the offhand way he began his response — ducking his head self-deprecatingly and saying, "There you go again" — that "won" the debate for Reagan.

Reagan wrapped up the campaign winningly — again, on television — by asking the American people if they were confident in the economy, secure in their jobs, satisfied with high inflation and interest rates, certain that the nation was strong and the world stable, and, most important, happier than they were before Carter became president. Few could answer yes to that question.

But much that had happened on Carter's watch was beyond his control. The most hurtful issue was the fate of 52 hostages held by Iran — America's avowed enemy since Muslim fundamentalists overthrew the murderous and American-backed shah in 1979. Carter had worked diligently and obsessively to obtain their release. He had even tried to free them with military force, an effort which had failed dismally, with American soldiers dying in a helicopter crash in the desert. Still, he could not pull off a much-hoped-for "September surprise," or an October surprise, or a November one. Reagan claimed he would have handled the hostage crisis differently but never became specific about what he would have done.

Specifics did not matter. Carter had preached the gospel of limits on American power and enunciated what was felt to be an American "malaise." Americans much preferred Reagan's optimistic assertions of a limitless American future. Even Carter's prescient prediction that Reagan's proposed economic policies would lead to a $130 billion deficit by 1983, a bloated establishment, and a federal government "stripped, impoverished and paralyzed for years to come" was of no avail. Reagan won with 50.7 percent of the vote, a plurality of 8.4 million. His electoral college victory was massive: 489 votes to Carter's 44.

The front page of the *New York Times* announces Reagan's inauguration and the release of the 52 American hostages by their Iranian captors on January 21, 1981. The Iranian hostage crisis was a key factor in Carter's demise and, thus, Reagan's ascendancy.

Was Reagan's victory a mandate? Probably not. Republican John Anderson had run a third-party campaign, drawing more votes from Carter than from Reagan. Without Anderson's intervention, Carter might have won. Moreover, only 26.7 percent of eligible voters had turned out on election day in 1980. And a CBS News–*New York Times* poll showed that only 11 percent of voters sampled voted for Reagan because of his conservative positions. A full 38 percent of Reagan's "supporters" had voted for him not because they believed in the man or his policies but rather only because he was an alternative to Carter.

6

The Biggest Screen

Once the Reagan team was installed in Washington and the task of making key appointments presented itself, President Reagan remained distant, generally preferring to let his millionaire backers make recommendations for him. As a result, appointments to Reagan's cabinet were made to reward friends, return political favors, and further business interests. For example, William French Smith, Reagan's personal lawyer and a man with very little experience in criminal law, became attorney general. Despite his lack of credentials, Smith was appointed mainly because he was a close friend of the president and had been instrumental in setting up Reagan's most lucrative real estate deals. Caspar Weinberger, who had worked with Reagan in California, was made secretary of defense, although his qualifications were as dubious as Smith's. The new secretary of state was Alexander

The president gives one of his weekly radio addresses. Aware that Reagan was much better at following a script than he was at responding to questions at impromptu meetings, the president's aides kept press conferences to a minimum during his years in office.

President Reagan and Vice-president George Bush sit for a portrait of the first Reagan cabinet. Most prominent were Secretary of State Alexander Haig and Secretary of Defense Caspar Weinberger (both seated), and (in the back row from left) Chief of Staff Donald Regan (second), Budget Director David Stockman (third), Secretary of the Interior James Watt (sixth), White House counsel Edwin Meese (seventh), and (standing, far right) CIA director William Casey.

Haig, a military man who had served as Nixon's chief of staff during the Watergate crisis and subsequently as the head of the North Atlantic Treaty Organization's armed forces. Donald Regan, who had run a major Wall Street brokerage firm, was made secretary of the Treasury. William Casey—who had been a top agent in the OSS (the Office of Strategic Services, the World War II precursor of the CIA), had become rich as a tax lawyer, had served Nixon in the State Department and as head of the Securities and Exchange Commission, and finally had become Reagan's campaign manager, replacing John Sears — became the new director of the CIA. Jeane Kirkpatrick, named UN ambassador, was the

only woman in the cabinet. Samuel Pierce, who became director of Housing and Urban Development, was the only black appointee.

The appointees wielding most power were Chief of Staff James Baker, formerly Bush's campaign manager; Edwin Meese, whose position as legal counsel to the president was upgraded to cabinet rank; and Michael Deaver, Reagan's old piano-playing buddy, who served as communications director and wielded unusual power because of his closeness to Reagan. These three determined the agenda of the executive branch by controlling access to the president. James B. Edwards, secretary of energy, was the least-qualified cabinet member, but Reagan had promised to abolish the Energy Department anyway. Secretary of the Interior James Watt — whose record showed him as antagonistic to the environment — was the most conservative appointee. Ultraconservatives, who had expected a decidedly rightward tilt in Reagan's appointments, were sorely disappointed. The far-right elements of the Republican party were relegated, for the most part, to minor positions in the Reagan administration.

Reagan, now nearly 70, was inaugurated on January 20, 1981. That morning, he joked with Deaver that he would have caught another hour or so of sleep had he not had an important engagement. This was in sharp contrast to President Carter, who during his final hours as president had stayed up all night in a frantic effort to arrange the release of the American hostages held by Iran for 444 days. Minutes after Reagan took office, the hostages were freed. The cost was the release of $8 billion in Iranian assets frozen in American banks.

The multi-million-dollar inaugural bash that ushered in the Reagan era was even more elaborate and costly than the one the Walt Disney Studios had dreamed up for Governor Reagan, setting the tone of the administration — flaunted wealth. In fact, the lavish affair might have been mistaken for a coronation were it not common knowledge that the United States was a republic.

Reagan's clear intention to steer clear of making executive decisions was demonstrated when aides presented him with a list of proposed accomplishments for the administration's first 100 days. He accepted the plan without a single question.

On March 30, the plan was almost thwarted by an assassin. John Hinckley, a mentally disturbed youth from Colorado, was so influenced by a violent character in the Martin Scorcese film *Taxi Driver* and so infatuated with the young actress Jodie Foster, one of the film's stars, that he, like the lead character in the film (played by Robert DeNiro) would have tried anything to impress her. As Reagan strode toward his limousine after speaking at the Washington Hilton, Hinckley fired several shots

> *[The president] sent out no strong signals. It was a rare meeting in which he made a decision or issued an order.*
> —DONALD REGAN
> Reagan's chief of staff

at the president. Press Secretary James Brady was wounded in the head. Reagan took a bullet in the chest and was rushed to the hospital.

Weak as he was with pain and loss of blood, Reagan managed a couple of one-liners while in the hospital. "Honey, I forgot to duck," he told his wife, and when wheeled into the operating room, he looked up at the surgeons and quipped, "Please tell me you're Republicans." His wounds were serious, but he had remarkable powers of recovery. He was soon released from the hospital and suffered only minor, temporary ill effects from the shooting. In fact, the attempt on his life proved to be a political blessing for Reagan: Once back in the saddle, the president enjoyed increased stature and a useful measure of conciliation from the press, the public, and both houses of Congress.

Secret Service officers react to the sound of gunfire on a Washington street. The Reagan era nearly came to an abrupt end on March 30, 1981, when a young drifter named John Hinckley fired six shots at the president. One bullet hit Reagan under the arm and lodged within an inch of his heart.

President and Mrs. Reagan leave George Washington Hospital on the day of his release. Reflecting on the assassination attempt, Reagan quoted British prime minister Winston Churchill: "There's no more exhilarating feeling than being shot at without result."

It had been decided that the economic agenda would take precedence over everything in the Reagan administration. On his first day in office, Reagan ordered an immediate hiring freeze with respect to federal employees. On February 17, he issued Executive Order 12291, giving control of the implementation of laws (a Congressional responsibility) to the Office of Management and Budget (OMB), headed by supply-side devotee David Stockman. OMB was thus allowed to veto — secretly — any regulation for which it deemed potential costs to outweigh potential benefits. Congressionally approved spending could thereby be stymied by low-level bureaucrats — the ultra-right-wing appointees so disappointed by Reagan's conservative but more moderate cabinet.

The Reagan administration's tendency to shroud its work in secrecy and tolerate those in government who played fast and loose with the law was demonstrated frequently. On April 15, the White House pardoned two high-level FBI officials previously convicted of ordering the illegal search of the homes of antiwar activists. Reagan claimed the agents had acted "on high principles." In late April, the White House stopped the preparation and printing of government publications, purportedly to eliminate waste but effectively impeding the flow of information on government activities. Agencies of the executive branch were ordered to evade laws designed to provide public accountability. New regulations were issued as "guidelines" to avoid public notification. Existing regulations were rewritten secretly.

The Freedom of Information Act — for years the best way for Americans to gain access to information about less-publicized government policies and activities — was weakened, first by the attorney general, next by a revision of the law. The Health and Human Services Department in June 1981 proposed that its activities be exempt from review by the courts. A presidential directive of January 12, 1982, expanded the definition of classified information, and on January 7, 1983, the government increased prohibitively the cost of obtaining information.

Tens of thousands of government officials were forced secretly to sign away the right to reveal "sensitive compartmentalized information." Thousands involved in government-funded research were denied the right to publish their results without government approval. Federally funded not-for-profit organizations were prohibited from taking political stands. Federal employees were subjected to polygraph tests in a hopeless attempt to stop unauthorized "leaks" of information. Three award-winning Canadian films about acid rain and nuclear war were defined as "political propaganda" under the 1938 Foreign Agents Registration Act and banned from the United States. Visas were denied to Mrs. Salvador Allende, wife of the slain Chilean

To me, the White House was as mysterious as a ghost ship; you heard the creak of the rigging and the groan of the timbers, and sometimes you even glimpsed the crew on the deck. But which of the crew had the helm? It was impossible to tell.
—ALEXANDER HAIG
Reagan's first secretary
of state

president, and the Colombian novelist Gabriel García Márquez.

The Reagan White House also took steps to impede the gathering of information. OMB planned budget cuts for programs monitoring the environment, gathering social data, and ensuring compliance with laws. Publications on welfare, child nutrition, labor statistics, housing, and occupational health hazards, as well as studies of nursing homes, medical expenses, and comparative U.S.-Soviet military spending were eliminated or curtailed.

While trying to keep the people uninformed, the Reagan administration took extraordinary steps to increase surveillance, through the National Recipient Information System of secret files on 20 million Americans receiving government benefits and the FBI's Interstate Identification Index of files on 40 million Americans with arrest records. The White House negotiated secretly with the House and Senate Intelligence Committee to authorize CIA spying on American citizens, a violation of the CIA charter. The Justice Department issued guidelines allowing the FBI to infiltrate any group, with or without cause. Pretrial detention—which would punish suspected criminals before they were convicted of a crime—was enacted in 1984.

After doing away with the Council on Wage and Price Stability, suspending 199 regulations issued after the election, and creating a task force on regulatory relief chaired by Bush, the president proposed $35 billion in budget cuts: these included elimination of the Comprehensive Employment Training Act and its public service jobs; an end to Social Security college benefits; the reduction of unemployment insurance from 39 to 26 weeks (even as the jobless rolls grew); the disappearance of $18 billion from the health budget (mainly from Medicare); and the elimination of disability payments to 1 million Americans. Aid to Families with Dependent Children would be drastically reduced. States would receive cuts in federal funding averaging 25 percent, forcing them to raise taxes. Even tax collection monies would be axed.

Reagan and Meese maintained, in all seriousness,

that there was no "authoritative" evidence of hunger in America, that people went to soup kitchens simply to take advantage of the free food. As a result, child nutrition programs, including meals for impoverished schoolchildren, were cut, and catsup was upgraded to vegetable status — in combination with French fries or hamburgers. Some $2 billion was cut from the food stamp program, reducing food expenditures for the poorest Americans.

Yet none of these cuts would reduce the federal deficit because entitlement programs such as Social Security — which could not be touched — absorbed 48 percent of the federal budget, and Reagan proposed massive defense budget increases that more than offset budget cuts. Some $49 billion would get the ball rolling, and for the next 5 years military expenditures would grow 7 percent a year.

Reagan also supported the Kemp-Roth bill to reduce income taxes 10 percent a year for 3 years. Estimates were that each of the richest 1 million U.S. households would gain more than $8,000 a year, while each of the poorest 19 million would lose $390.

With the national debt approaching $1 trillion, David Stockman — the budget wizard — backed plans to raise the Social Security retirement age and lower minimum benefits. This proved politically unacceptable and resulted in an independent commission to make Social Security fiscally sound.

President Reagan took to the airwaves to drum up support for these proposals, and on May 7 the Democratic-controlled House of Representatives passed the budget. By July 29, the tax cuts were voted into law. On September 24, the president made a nationally televised appeal for an additional $13 billion in budget cuts, but by December economists forecast that the fiscal shortfall would top $109 billion in 1982 anyway, and rise thereafter — this effectively ended Reagan's campaign pledge to balance the budget by 1984.

The business community doubted the wisdom of Reagan's economic policies, even when offered sweeping reductions in corporate income taxes. The stock market tumbled. Consumers decided to spend

— rather than invest — the money that tax breaks allowed them to keep from the government. The resulting deep recession produced the highest unemployment rate in 40 years, with 11 million out of work by 1982. The recession — and some creative bookkeeping — did lower inflation, but at the expense of the highest poverty rate in 20 years, the highest prime interest lending rates in history, and gargantuan budget deficits.

Reagan refused to acknowledge the connection between his policies and the recession, but in a December 1981 interview in the *Atlantic Monthly*, Stockman admitted that budget figures had been contrived to provide impossibly optimistic results and that supply-side theory could not work.

The economy would not revive until 1983, when the cartel controlling worldwide oil supplies cut prices due to falling demand. Not until 1984 would Reagan consider new deficit-reducing taxes, and then only because the word *tax* was avoided: $14 billion in corporate taxes were called "closing loopholes" and surcharges on gasoline were labeled "user fees." In his State of the Union address on January 25, 1984, Reagan called for another $100 billion in budget cuts.

The Reagan administration's preference for corporate management over workers was demonstrated most blatantly by the air traffic controllers' strike of August 3, 1981. When some 13,000 controllers employed by the Department of Transportation defied the government's back-to-work order, Reagan, onetime union leader and now union buster, fired them all and decertified their union. Subsequently there was a dramatic increase in air traffic accidents and fatalities. Firms were allowed to cancel labor agreements by moving from union to nonunion plants or to void contracts by declaring bankruptcy (as Continental Airlines did, laying off half its workers and cutting wages 50 percent). A subsequent Labor Department rule change allowed state employment agencies to supply scab labor during strikes, further weakening unions.

Meanwhile, Reagan did nothing to help the cause of women's rights. Possibly influenced by the lob-

Douglas Fraser, president of the United Auto Workers union, joins striking air traffic controllers on a picket line at Detroit's Metro Airport in August 1981. When the workers refused to abandon their strike and obey a government back-to-work order, Reagan fired them and busted the union.

byists of the religious Right, which had helped him get elected, Reagan had taken a hard-line antichoice position on the abortion issue. Furthermore, as 2.5 million women slipped below the poverty line by 1984, they watched the defeat of the Equal Rights Amendment after a 10-year fight for its passing. The defeat of the bill, due in no small measure to Reagan's opposition to it, was a hard blow against women in their struggle for fair recognition and compensation in the workplace. What little support Reagan had had among American women dwindled even further. In July 1981, he named the first woman justice to the Supreme Court, Sandra Day O'Connor, but this appointment did little to narrow the gender gap in Reagan's approval rating.

In July 1981, under pressure from women's groups for his antichoice position on the abortion issue and his opposition to the Equal Rights Amendment, Reagan nominated a 51-year-old Arizona Court of Appeals judge, Sandra Day O'Connor, to serve on the Supreme Court of the United States. She became the first female justice to sit on the Court in its 192-year history.

Blacks and other minorities — disproportionately afflicted by Reaganomics — were astonished in 1982 when the attorney general supported restoration of tax-exempt status to 100 racially segregated schools and again in 1983 when Reagan opposed strengthening the Voting Rights Act. Affirmative action to increase minority employment and bilingual education was slashed, and the Reagan administration attacked voluntary as well as mandatory school busing to achieve integration. Worse still, when the U.S. Commission on Civil Rights reported in October 1983 that the enforcement of civil rights laws had dropped precipitously, Reagan took the unprecedented step of firing three commissioners and replacing them with conservatives. One such appointee, chairman Clarence Pendleton, who claimed that the groups most victimized by discrimination were Eastern Europeans, and staff director Linda Chavez, who persuaded the commission to study reverse discrimination — whites adversely affected by affirmative action — instead of the negative impact of the Reagan budget cuts. Administration support for the Union of South Africa, which held its black majority in bondage, came as no surprise.

A disturbing example of Reagan's view of minority groups was his failure to react to the epidemic of the deadly acquired immune deficiency syndrome (AIDS). By the mid-1980s, the fatal disease, spread primarily through sexual activity and contaminated needles, was having a disastrous effect on America's homosexual population, its urban poor, and its minority black community, in which there could be found a high percentage of intravenous drug abusers. Even while the virus infiltrated the nation's heterosexual population and became the American people's chief health concern, the issue was a low priority on the Reagan administration's agenda. The president was criticized in the media for his insensitivity on the AIDS issue, and demonstrations across the country underscored public dismay over his inaction. Still, Reagan took no initiative to provide the needed additional funding for AIDS research and education, possibly in part because many of the president's longtime supporters were hard-line Christians who condemned homosexuals. Only when his old friend actor Rock Hudson died of the disease did Reagan show any sign of sensitivity on the AIDS issue.

On the environmental front, the motives of the Reagan administration were questionable as well. Although James Watt, secretary of the interior, was the administrator in charge of safeguarding the environment, he sought to give corporate America every advantage for making profits even at the expense the environment. A friend of the oil industry, Watt planned to make 1 billion acres of coastal lands — more than 10 times the size of existing tracts — available for offshore oil drilling. He declared a moratorium on national park acquisition and sought to open federally protected wilderness areas for development before Congress stopped him. Finally, in late 1981, Watt was called to task for his outlandish disrespect for America's natural environment: The Sierra Club, an important environmental group, gathered more than 1 million signatures demanding his dismissal while concerned citizens and many journalists called for Watt's resignation.

> *We will mine more, drill more, cut more timber.*
> —JAMES WATT
> Reagan's first secretary of the interior

The Reagans appear on stage with the Beach Boys, one of Mrs. Reagan's favorite musical groups, during a concert in 1983. When Secretary of the Interior James Watt — not a Beach Boys fan — criticized the group's music and life-style, he was reproved by the first lady.

Reagan stood behind Watt, even through the summer of 1982, when the beleaguered interior secretary, in a moment of gross and outrageous indiscretion, warned Jewish Americans that any opposition on their part to administration energy policies could strain relations with Israel. But in the fall of 1983, when Watt referred to his coal-mining advisory panel as "a black, a woman, two Jews, and a cripple," it was obvious he simply had to go.

Watt was not the Reagan administration's only blight on the environment. The OMB examined a

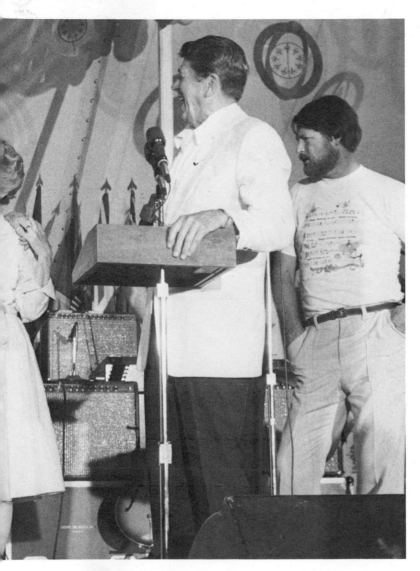

national toxic waste cleanup proposal and con-
cluded that it would be too costly to save American
lives through the elimination of toxic sludge and
cancer-causing chemicals. Their statistical analysis
factored in the value of a human life, which they
estimated to be $22,500. The OMB's cost analyses
of Environmental Protection Agency (EPA) programs caused environmental action to grind to a
virtual halt. And in May 1982, the Nuclear Regulatory Commission secretly suspended safety
regulations.

Billions of dollars in a "superfund" to clean up the nation's worst toxic dump sites went undisbursed, and when Congress sought information, Reagan instructed EPA administrator Anne Gorsuch to withhold "enforcement-sensitive" documents from Congress. Congress sought a compromise, but when Gorsuch fired an EPA economist who refused to falsify Clean Air Act costs, Congress cited her for contempt—a first for a cabinet official.

In response, the Reagan Justice Department filed suit against House subpoenas, a suit subsequently dismissed by the Supreme Court as meritless. When

Protesters outside the White House demonstrate their dissatisfaction with the Reagan administration's policy on AIDS, a fatal disease that strikes at the immune system, which reached epidemic proportions during the 1980s. One AIDS activist, the president's son Ronald, appeared on a televised public service announcement urging citizens and public officials to respond to the pressing need for more AIDS research and education.

a congressman demanded "the right" to question Rita Lavelle, an EPA administrator in charge of the toxic dump cleanup program, Reagan fired her, causing such an uproar that he was forced to ask the Justice Department to investigate the EPA. Even during the investigation, the White House fired two additional EPA officials. When the investigation revealed too cozy a relationship between the EPA and corporate polluters, the White House turned on Gorsuch.

Meanwhile, Reagan continued to be out of touch. For example, on August 19, 1981, when American

F-14 fighter planes were attacked by two Russian-built Libyan jets and shot them down, nobody woke the sleeping Reagan to tell him about it.

The few initiatives Reagan did take, particularly in foreign affairs, were often ill conceived and poorly executed. For instance, influenced by CIA chief William Casey — once described as "the last great buccaneer from OSS" — Reagan called for a privately funded, White House–controlled "Project Democracy" in an address to the British Parliament on June 8, 1982. Project Democracy would be an unofficial CIA, run by the National Security Council, free of Congressional oversight. This extralegal entity was brought into existence in January 1983, when Reagan signed National Security Directive 77. What cause would Project Democracy serve? The so-called Reagan Doctrine — enunciated in that same address to Parliament. Theorizing that the Soviet Union was "inherently unstable," Reagan hoped the United States and its allies would use any means, covert or otherwise, to exploit this instability and assist in the Soviet Union's downfall.

Reagan had previously fulfilled another campaign promise — over Secretary Haig's objection — by lifting the Soviet grain embargo. On November 18, 1981, he offered the Soviets his arms control agreement: The United States would not deploy a new generation of intermediate-range nuclear forces (INF) in Europe if the Soviets would dismantle all of their prepositioned INF launchers. This so-called zero option was an obvious ploy to force both Congress and reluctant Europeans to proceed with the installation of American Pershing missiles on European soil because the Soviets would not trade something for nothing. Nevertheless, the Soviets opened INF talks with the United States in Geneva on November 30.

The proposed deployment of Pershing missiles led to an international, citizen-initiated protest, the nuclear freeze movement, which sought to "freeze" nuclear weapons in place and begin negotiations for their elimination. Reagan called the freeze "dangerous" because it could give the Soviet Union military superiority.

On May 9, 1982, under pressure from the public,

Congress, and his image-sensitive wife, Reagan introduced START — the Strategic Arms Reduction Talks. Although Reagan sought to reduce the number of ballistic missile warheads, his plan would have allowed the United States to continue developing its arsenal while the Soviets reduced theirs by half.

These START proposals were hard to take seriously from the man who regularly condemned the Soviet Union as "the evil empire" and who could blithely warm up before one of his regular Saturday afternoon radio broadcasts — his ongoing version of Roosevelt's Fireside Chats — by quipping that we would begin "bombing Moscow in five minutes." The Soviet Union rejected Reagan's plan.

On June 12, 1982, the nuclear freeze movement climaxed with the largest demonstration in American history when 750,000 marchers rallied at the United Nations, which was holding a special session on disarmament. At the end of that month, Soviet leader Brezhnev agreed to new arms reduction talks in Geneva.

On June 24, 1982, a battle-weary Alexander Haig resigned. His replacement as secretary of state, George Shultz, had a long-standing rivalry with Secretary of Defense Caspar Weinberger that led to virtual paralysis at the White House level, allowing subordinates to exercise unusual control in foreign affairs.

START negotiations began in earnest on July 29, 1982, but the talks were slowed when Brezhnev died on November 10; they were sidetracked again by the introduction of SDI in March 1983 and further stalled on August 31, 1983, when a Korean jetliner carrying 269 passengers was shot down after straying hundreds of miles into Soviet air space and passing suspiciously over sensitive military facilities. Then Brezhnev's successor, Yuri Andropov, died on February 9, 1984, after a long illness, causing further delays in the talks.

There was also trouble for Reagan in the Middle East, especially in war-torn Lebanon. After the September 16, 1982, massacre of innocent people in the Sabra and Shatilla refugee camps, an action

A U.S. Marine holds the seal of the United States that was part of the American Embassy in Beirut, Lebanon, before it was bombed by Muslim terrorists in April 1983. Forty-seven people were killed in the explosion.

condoned by invading Israeli forces, 1,200 U.S. Marines were posted to the exposed airport in Beirut, the Lebanese capital, with no clear mission. On April 18, 1983, a car bomb blew up the U.S. Embassy in Beirut, killing 47. Two marines were killed and 14 wounded by a Muslim mortar attack on Beirut airport on August 29. The civil war in Lebanon worsened, and in September five more marines were killed. On September 8, a U.S. warship shelled Muslim positions, and on September 13, Reagan authorized a full naval bombardment. The results were devastating. On October 23, a suicide driver rammed a truck full of explosives into the main U.S. Marine barracks at Beirut airport, killing 241 servicemen.

Confronted with this terrible tragedy, Reagan refused to interrupt a golfing weekend. Two days later, he ordered marines and U.S. Rangers to invade the tiny Caribbean nation of Grenada, a Communist country suffering internal turmoil that supposedly threatened American students studying there. The Reagan administration imposed complete press censorship on the military operation in Grenada. Subsequent images of returning students kissing U.S. soil confirmed Americans' delight in the victory. With this almost risk-free and possibly need-less offensive, Reagan deflected attention from the mass murder in Beirut. The press, by now predict-ably, followed Reagan's lead.

On February 26, 1984, Reagan quietly removed the marines from Lebanon. This led to the abduc-tion of Americans by Lebanese factions sympathetic to Iran. American relations with Iran had deterio-rated during Iran's territorial war with neighboring Iraq when American ships were ordered into the Persian Gulf to keep vital oil-shipping lanes open.

The United States was also involved in Central American wars. Since the 1979 overthrow of Nica-ragua's American-backed dictator Anastasio So-moza, the ruling Sandinistas — leftists supported by Cuba and the Soviet Union — had been opposed by American-backed rebels known as the contras. The contra cause became the Reagan administration's crusade. In mid-February 1982, Americans were shocked to learn that the CIA was training the con-tras. Fearing that the United States might suffer defeat in the jungles of Nicaragua as it had in Viet-nam, Congress passed the Boland amendment in December 1983, explicitly forbidding U.S. aid for the overthrow of the Nicaraguan government.

Despite the provisions of the Boland amendment, 5,000 CIA-trained and -supplied contras entered Nicaragua on April 3, 1983. U.S. support for violent regimes in El Salvador and Honduras helpful to the contras continued, and a secret airfield in Costa Rica was constructed in an effort to more easily sup-ply the contras with military aid. On April 27, 1983, Reagan appeared before a joint session of Congress to plead unsuccessfully for bipartisan support for his Central American policies. One year later, when the CIA was forced to acknowledge its illegal mining of Nicaraguan harbors, Congress strengthened the Boland amendment.

In the meantime Reagan's personal net worth in-creased to an estimated $5 million. He proudly showed off his 4 new pairs of $1,000 cowboy boots for the media even as the country suffered through a recession and the number of homeless Americans and children being born with AIDS climbed.

They are the moral equal of the Founding Fathers and the brave men and women of the French Resistance. We cannot turn away from them. For the struggle here is not right versus left, but right versus wrong.
—RONALD REAGAN
on the Nicaraguan contras

A homeless woman, carrying her few possessions in two torn shopping bags, meanders through the streets of New York. During the 1980s, the number of homeless Americans increased dramatically while the Reagan administration simply ignored the problem or denied that there was one.

His family life, however, was not ideal. In particular, his relationship with his children — except for Maureen — was strained. For instance, Ronald, who shocked his family by becoming a ballet dancer and appearing in his underwear on the television show "Saturday Night Live," publicly criticized his father's inaction on the AIDS problem, and Patricia, whose political views were as far to the left as her father's were to the right, eventually wrote a thinly veiled exposé of the Reagan White House that was extremely critical of her parents.

The Reagan gaffes of his first term became more frequent in his second. For example, he told Israeli prime minister Yitzhak Shamir, and subsequently Nazi-hunter Simon Wiesenthal, that he had filmed the Nazi death camps at the end of World War II when in fact he had never left the country before making a movie in England in 1949.

But Americans continued to love their president no matter what, or, when angered, they would quickly forgive him. Reagan was called the Teflon President because criticism — and responsibility — seemed to slide right off him. Eventually, Reagan was so popular that nobody even dared to criticize him. In particular, the news media, traditionally relied on to provide a critical perspective on government policy and programs, gave Reagan a seemingly endless holiday.

Nancy Reagan fared less well under public scrutiny. Many criticized her for what they perceived as her inappropriate extravagance. They were offended by her expensive clothes, her purchasing of White House china for $209,508, and her spending $822,641 on redecorating the White House. That most of these luxuries had been paid for by the Reagans' rich friends did not make these material indulgences any less exorbitant. While there were those who were not bothered by the first lady's free spending, many Americans thought she was simply self-flattering. Some even considered her spendthrift ways an insult to the working people of America and the family values to which the Republicans so often paid lip service, not to mention America's poor.

> *As a rule, I did not think it was lying to suggest that the president might be aware of something when he wasn't.*
> —LARRY SPEAKES
> Reagan's press secretary

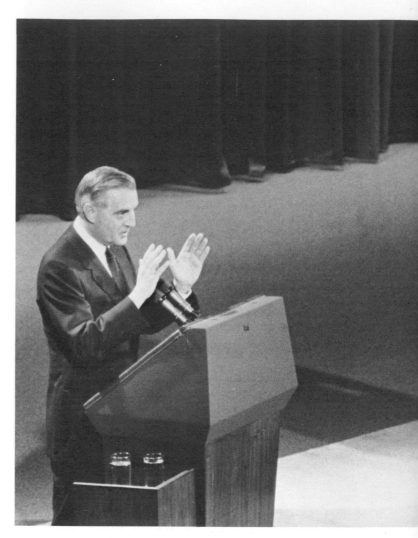

Vice-president under Jimmy Carter and the Democratic nominee for president in 1984, Walter Mondale debates the issues with Reagan in Louisville, Kentucky. Mondale, who accused Reagan of presiding over a social movement based on greed and aimed at enriching the few at the expense of the many, lost the election in a landslide.

The 1984 election was no contest. The Democratic challenger, Walter Mondale, Jimmy Carter's vice-president, named Geraldine Ferraro as his running mate. Thus, she became the first woman to run for the office. But Ferraro proved burdensome when her husband's shady real estate deals came to light. Mondale almost ended the campaign before it began by calling for new taxes. Even if new taxes were needed, Americans did not want to hear about it. Rather, they preferred the optimistic slogans of the feel-good candidate Reagan, who assured them that the best was still to come. "It's morning in America," he told them.

Reagan stumbled badly in his first debate with Mondale, appearing absentminded, confused, and ill informed. But he was better prepared for the second debate. As 100 million Americans watched, Reagan waited for the perfect opportunity to launch his best joke — announcing that he would not make age a campaign issue, refusing to exploit his opponent's youth and inexperience. It was classic Reagan, and the American people ate it up.

In the general election, Reagan defeated Mondale more soundly than he had Carter. Carter had won in several states, but Mondale carried only his home state of Minnesota.

7

Presidency II: The Sequel

On January 7, 1985, Donald Regan and James Baker switched jobs. The idea was their own, and Regan — the new chief of staff — was astonished by the president's acquiescence. He was even more astonished when he presented his plan for Reagan's second term and learned what others had learned before him: Reagan accepted almost any suggestion from his staff—without emendation.

By the middle of Reagan's second term, more than 100 members of the White House staff had resigned. Some hoped to use their connections in the federal government to make money in the private sector, and others were forced out under allegations of wrongdoing. National Security Adviser Richard Allen, for instance, left office because he had accepted

> *I believe that you surround yourself with the best people you can find, delegate authority, and don't interfere.*
> —RONALD REAGAN

Members of the International Ladies' Garment Workers' Union protest the Reagan administration's hands-off policy regarding imports. During the Reagan years, many manufacturing jobs were lost as U.S. companies discovered cheap labor abroad and little or no customs limits on goods imported for retail.

The president and first lady say a tearful good-bye to White House aide Michael Deaver, who left his post in early 1985 to work as a political consultant. Later, he was prosecuted for influence peddling and was eventually convicted of perjury before a congressional investigating committee.

illegal gratuities — 2 watches and $1,000 — on Mrs. Reagan's behalf, the day after Reagan's first inauguration. Secretary of Labor Raymond Donovan took a leave of absence in the fall of 1984 because of reputed ties to organized crime and resigned on March 15, 1985, after being formally charged with defrauding the New York City Transit Authority of $7.4 million. (Later acquitted, Donovan was the first sitting cabinet officer ever to be indicted on criminal charges.) Lyn Nofziger — once Governor Reagan's communications director — had served in the White House political wing and was convicted, after resigning, of influence peddling (though the conviction was later overturned). Michael Deaver too

— who left his post in early 1985 to seek riches as a political consultant — was prosecuted for influence peddling and eventually convicted of perjury before a congressional investigating committee.

Soon it became public that some members of Reagan's administration were involved in questionable financial dealings. For example, William Smith — the attorney general, who should have known better — made profitable tax-shelter investments outside of the blind trust designed to protect him from undue influence. Caspar Weinberger and William Casey had not even bothered to put their assets into blind trusts, and Casey omitted significant items from his legally required financial disclosure forms.

None of these disreputable doings bothered Reagan, but his presidency was damaged by similar improprieties on the part of Edwin Meese, revealed during the brutalizing Senate confirmation hearings that finally led to Meese's replacement of Smith as attorney general. When Meese was implicated in the spring of 1987 in a scandal involving the Wedtech Corporation, a military subcontractor, he had to appoint a special prosecutor to investigate 11 separate charges against him, ranging from favorable financial dealings with individuals who later received lucrative federal appointments to irregularities in his financial disclosure reports. Meese would spend most of his term as attorney general hampered and ineffective and would finally resign under mounting pressure and public outrage in July 1988.

Reagan's vaunted military buildup was also a source of financial wrongdoing. On December 2, 1985, the General Dynamics Corporation was indicted for defrauding the army. That was just part of a pattern of abuse of a defense budget that had risen to almost $300 billion annually — including such price gouging as a 12-cent Allen wrench that cost the military $9,600 and plastic caps for chair legs purchased for $1,000 each.

It seemed Reagan's second term would be business as usual, if not a rerun of the first. Family farms — squeezed by merciless federal loan agencies — were disappearing at the rate of 180 per day. Corporate mergers were occurring—with little antitrust analysis — 4 times as frequently as in 1984, 20 times the rate before Reagan's presidency. U.S. trade deficits to Japan continued to grow. More manufacturing jobs disappeared — beyond the 1.6 million lost since 1980 — and of the many jobs created by Reagan's economic "miracle," 90 percent paid less than $14,000 a year and 60 percent less than $7,000. The earnings gap between the poorest 40 percent of Americans and the richest 40 percent was the widest since the Census Bureau started tracking such figures in 1947.

The national debt was approaching $2 trillion, so Reagan had to establish priorities and make some

> *The aides in close contact with President Reagan today are the least distinguished such group to serve any president in the postwar period.*
>
> —GEORGE WILL
> syndicated columnist

tough decisions. He proposed more budget cuts —
$2.7 billion from Medicare and civil service retire-
ment programs, $3 billion from Aid to Families with
Dependent Children (AFDC) and food stamps, and
$3 billion more from other domestic programs, but
requested another increase — $29 billion — for de-
fense. While Reagan praised Americans' spirit of vol-
untarism, he proposed the abolition of tax
deductions for charitable contributions by most
taxpayers.

When Reagan, in his 1985 State of the Union mes-
sage, called for a "Second American Revolution of
hope and opportunity," the phrase had a bitter ring.
In March, his Justice Department continued its assault on the electorate's right to know by seeking
permission to use the 1917 Espionage Act to make
giving classified information to the American people
a crime.

The stated "major initiative" of Reagan's second
term was the revised tax code proposed in May 1985,
designed in part to close loopholes and eliminate
tax breaks but also to reduce the highest federal tax
rates from 50 to 28 percent. Since the regressive
Social Security tax (set at the same rate for all wage
earners, regardless of income) was rising, this tax
package would further benefit the rich at the expense of the poor and middle class. Moreover, the
new tax provisions would not curb the ever-ex-
panding federal deficit because Reagan insisted
that any changes to the tax code be "revenue neu-
tral" — that is, they could not alter the amount of
tax income, only the sources. Congress tried to do
something about the deficit by passing the Gramm-
Rudman-Hollings budget reduction law on December 11, 1985, requiring across-the-board budget
cuts if specified deficit reduction targets were not
met. As if to mock the new law, the Pentagon declared the unimaginably costly SDI its highest priority on December 31.

Reagan took flight from these domestic troubles,
literally, to such international photo opportunities
as the annual economic summit meetings with leaders of the major Western industrial nations. He glo-
ried in his stirring and solemn trip to France on the

Don't bring me problems—
bring me solutions.
—RONALD REAGAN

40th anniversary of D day — the assault that marked the beginning of the end for Nazi Germany.

But even the best stage managers make mistakes, and Reagan's worst began in November 1984, when he accepted an invitation from West German chancellor Helmut Kohl — who had already clasped hands with French president François Mitterrand in a moving ceremony at the battlefield of Verdun — to come to a cemetery at Bitburg, Germany, to acknowledge the end of the bitterness engendered by two world wars. Kohl also recommended a visit to one of the death camps, but Reagan declined, perhaps fearful of reviving memories of his story of having filmed one.

What was not known at the time was that Bitburg contained the graves of 47 members of the Waffen SS — Nazi leader Adolf Hitler's elite guard. When this fact was discovered, Jewish and humanitarian groups worldwide were horrified and begged Reagan not to go. But Reagan felt compelled to fulfill his pledge, and to make up for this blunder he reluctantly scheduled a visit to Bergen-Belsen, the concentration camp in which diarist Anne Frank had died. No one was appeased by this gesture, which some considered an insult and others perceived as a desperate attempt at damage control.

During that same trip, in November 1985, Reagan was heckled at the World Parliament by demonstrators protesting U.S. policy in Nicaragua. Reagan responded by claiming the protestors did not know what they were talking about because they had not been to Nicaragua, and he had. Of course, he had not been there either.

The Reagan administration's grip on international affairs seemed to be slipping. On July 11, 1985, contrary to the administration's position, the Senate voted to impose economic sanctions on South Africa. In February 1986, Haiti's murderous "president for life," Jean-Claude Duvalier, was forced to flee a popular uprising in a U.S. Air Force jet. Later that same month, Reagan had to do an about-face on support for Philippine ruler Ferdinand Marcos, who sought asylum in Hawaii after

During a 1985 trip to West Germany, President Reagan pays his respects at the Bergen-Belsen memorial cemetery, where some of the countless victims of Nazi atrocities are buried. His visit was prompted by the controversy surrounding his prior visit to the cemetery at Bitburg, the burial place of several Nazi war criminals.

stealing an election from Corazon Aquino and remained there under house arrest until his death in 1989.

With the secretaries of state and defense at a stand-off, much responsibility for foreign affairs fell to Robert "Bud" McFarlane — a Vietnam veteran who had served as military assistant to Henry Kissinger and had become Reagan's national security adviser nine days after the Beirut airport massacre in October 1983. After a quiet first year, McFarlane became more aggressive, carefully crafting a list of foreign policy objectives. He was astounded when Reagan returned it with a single comment: "Let's do them all."

This willingness in large measure to leave the tough decisions to others led to the debacle known as Iran-contra, which crippled the remaining years of Reagan's presidency and undermined the foreign policy of the United States.

The nightmare began on July 3, 1985, when David Kimche, an Israeli espionage specialist, told McFarlane that — through a man named Manucher Ghorbanifar — a channel of communication between the United States and supposedly moderate elements of the Iranian leadership could be opened. If the United States would help Iran buy war matériel for its ongoing battle with Iraq, the Iranians would help free seven Americans held hostage in Lebanon.

Reagan first heard of the scheme while hospitalized for the removal of a cancerous growth from his colon. The hostages were an embarrassment to Reagan. Despite a pledge never to bargain with terrorists and despite "Operation Staunch" (announced by Secretary Shultz in December 1983) with which America tried to keep its allies from selling arms to Iran, Reagan was sufficiently intrigued by the notion of Iranian moderates and the hope of freeing the hostages to go against the strong protests of both Weinberger and Shultz and allow McFarlane to pursue the new initiative.

McFarlane had to proceed carefully. It was illegal for the United States to provide arms to terrorists, as the Iranian regime had been dubbed. But he and others in the administration thought that the U.S.

> *The charge has been made that the United States has shipped weapons to Iran as ransom payment for the release of American hostages in Lebanon; that the United States undercut its allies and secretly violated American policy against trafficking with terrorists. Those charges are absolutely false.*
>
> —RONALD REAGAN
> when the Iran-contra story
> first broke

government, by directing Israel to sell the desired TOW antitank missiles to Iran and later resupplying Israel, could accomplish its goal without violating the law.

A small arms delivery was made on August 20, 1985, but Iranian officials insisted no hostages would be released until all the TOW missiles had been received. A second shipment was made on September 14th, but the Iranians kept only part of their bargain: Only a single hostage would be freed, though the Americans could choose which one.

The choice was William Buckley, the CIA's Beirut station chief, who reportedly was being tortured. The Iranians sent back word that Buckley was "too ill" to be released (having died in captivity the preceding June) and set free the Reverend Benjamin Weir instead.

These bungled maneuvers should have made the Americans wary, but the Iranians wanted a further deal, this time offering to release a number of hostages for the purchase of HAWK antiaircraft missiles. Reagan — under pressure from the hostages' families — was becoming obsessive about their freedom and told McFarlane to proceed. In early November, McFarlane — whose nerves were rattled — put the operation into the hands of his aide Colonel Oliver North.

North, another Vietnam veteran, was a member of the National Security Council staff who had played an important role in the invasion of Grenada. Charged with keeping the contras armed despite the Boland amendment, he had become a zealous disciple of William Casey, the CIA chief, who provided advice, encouragement, and useful contacts. North shared Reagan's belief that the contras were the "moral equal of our Founding Fathers" and enlisted the aid of Carl Russell "Spitz" Channell to raise money for the contras from private sources. In the summer of 1985, North helped Richard Secord, an American, and Albert Hakim, an Iranian exile, both with long service in shady arms deals, set up a corporation to resupply the contras on a regular basis. In October, North distinguished himself by orchestrating the daring F-14 fighter jet interception of a

What began as a strategic opening to Iran deteriorated, in its implementation, into trading arms for hostages. It was a mistake.
—RONALD REAGAN

Marine Corps lieutenant colonel Oliver North appears before the Iran-contra committee on July 7, 1987. North's patriotic verve and maudlin sincerity during the hearings won over the American people and made him a media star. The Vietnam War hero was indicted on — and eventually convicted of — criminal charges.

plane carrying terrorists who had seized a cruise ship, the *Achille Lauro*, to escape from prison in Italy to Egypt. By November, he was gung ho to deal with the Iranians.

The November arms shipment was a failure on two counts: First, the Iranians were incensed that the weapons they received were obsolete — and marked with the Jewish star of David — and refused to release hostages; second, the mission had run into difficulties which caused North to involve CIA operatives, thus implicating America in the Iranian arms sales and forcing the president to sign an authorization.

Israeli arms dealer Al Schwimmer had given North $1 million to cover expenses for the mission, and when the deal fell through, he did not ask for the return of the remaining money — $850,000. Although there is much confusion as to who was responsible for conceiving the scheme, North used Schwimmer's money as the seed for Project Democracy, setting up a tangled series of Swiss bank accounts in which to stash funds from Saudi Arabia,

Israel, and Taiwan as well as to hide profits made by overcharging the Iranians in subsequent arms sales. These monies would be used primarily to fund the contras. North called bilking the Iranians to help the contras a "neat idea."

McFarlane resigned on December 4, 1985, to be replaced by Vice Admiral John Poindexter. Poindexter was most supportive of North's efforts.

In the meantime, on December 27, 1985, Palestinian terrorists killed 20 civilians at airports in Rome and Vienna. On January 7, 1986, Reagan publicly declared Libyan leader Muammar el-Qaddafi responsible. On April 5, terrorists blew up a discotheque in West Berlin, killing 1 American serviceman and injuring 60 others. Again Reagan blamed Qaddafi, whom he called a "mad dog." On April 14, Reagan ordered the bombing of the Libyan cities of Tripoli and Benghazi. Qaddafi's adopted infant daughter was killed and two of his sons injured in the raids.

Former national security adviser John Poindexter testifies before the Iran-contra committee on July 16, 1987. When it was revealed that Poindexter and North were selling arms to Iran and diverting the profits to the Nicaraguan rebels, Americans looked to the president for some explanation — but he had none.

Libyan men wade through the rubble following the U.S. air strike on Tripoli in April 1986. The Reagan administration stated that the U.S. attack on Libya was in retaliation for the terrorist acts sponsored by Libyan leader Muammar el-Qaddafi, who in the aftermath of the raid remarked, "That's what superpowers do."

On May 25, 1986, McFarlane joined North on a secret mission to the Iranian capital, Tehran, for direct negotiations. In addition to arms, they carried gifts: A cake decorated with a key, .357-caliber pistols, and a Bible inscribed by President Reagan. They soon discovered that there were no Iranian moderates — that they had been dealing with the Iranian leadership all along. McFarlane, convinced that the Iranians would continue to renege on their promises ("rug merchant stuff," as Donald Regan would later call it), became completely disillusioned. North remained enthusiastic, both because he had hopes for the release of the hostages and because the contras needed more money.

With the public still in the dark about any bargaining with Iran, Reagan's approval ratings soared after the bombing of Libya. Before the Fourth of July, Congress gave him $100 million for the contras, including $70 million in military aid.

July 4 also brought Reagan good news in the form of Chief Justice Warren Burger's retirement. This gave Reagan an opportunity to continue shifting the Supreme Court to the right by elevating conservative William Rehnquist to chief justice and appointing another conservative, Antonin Scalia, to fill Rehnquist's spot on the bench.

Despite funding from Congress, North continued his illicit support of the contras. In early October 1986, a supply plane was shot down in Nicaragua, and the only survivor — Eugene Hasenfus, formerly of the CIA — claimed that this was a government mission and that the flight had been supervised by the CIA. UPI and *New York Newsday* reported the discovery of telephone records that linked Hasenfus to Colonel North.

The whole Iran-contra mess was about to unravel. Since May, North had supervised two more arms sales to Iran and had been rewarded with the release of Father Lawrence Jenco in July and, in early November, David Jacobsen, director of the American University Hospital in Beirut. This might have indicated that the scheme was working, except that terrorists had abducted two more Americans in September.

At about the time of Jacobsen's release, a left-wing Lebanese magazine, *Al Shiraa*, broke the story of the secret North-McFarlane mission to Tehran. Within the week, the *Washington Post* and the *Los Angeles Times* were able to give detailed accounts of the Iranian arms deals. Before the November elections — in which Democrats increased their majority in the House of Representatives and regained control of the Senate — the scandal had gripped the nation.

On November 13, Reagan went on television, explaining that only small quantities of "defensive" weapons had been involved and absurdly insisting that all of the arms sold to Iran would have fit into a single cargo plane. During a November press conference, Reagan denied that the United States had condoned Israel's involvement in the arms shipment — a misstatement of fact that had to be corrected by the White House almost before Reagan left the room.

Reagan proceeded to put his own political spin on the affair, insisting that the arms sales were not an arms-for-hostages swap but rather a diplomatic effort to open relations with Iranian moderates. He

It was the president's policy— not an isolated decision by North or Poindexter—to sell arms secretly to Iran and to maintain the contras 'body and soul,' the Boland amendment notwithstanding. For failing to take care that the law reigned supreme, the president bears the responsibility.
—congressional committee's report on the Iran-contra scandal

also claimed to know nothing about the diversion of funds to the contras.

Attorney General Meese conducted a casual investigation, interviewing participants personally, rarely asking probing questions, and never taking notes. He also gave North and Poindexter plenty of opportunity to destroy damaging evidence. North, in particular, shredded documents and erased computer files fervently. Poindexter was forced out of office, and North was fired. In a commiserating telephone call, Reagan told North he was a hero and opined that his story would make a great movie someday.

Because the government was investigating itself, Meese reluctantly named Lawrence Walsh special prosecutor in the case. Reagan appointed Senators John Tower, Edmund Muskie, and Brent Scowcroft to a special commission to find out exactly what had happened. The Tower Commission, as it was called, faced many difficulties, not the least of which was 73-year-old William Casey's hospitalization with a malignant brain tumor in mid-December. Unable to speak, Casey took his knowledge to the grave on May 6, 1987.

McFarlane was more forthcoming, but on February 9, 1987, before his third scheduled round of questioning by the commission, he attempted suicide by swallowing 20 Valium pills. He survived, however, and proved a very valuable witness.

Perhaps the commission's most recalcitrant witness was Reagan himself. Time and again — as he had 25 years before, during the investigation of the MCA waiver — Reagan could not remember crucial information, such as signing the finding required by the November 1985 arms shipment — a document Poindexter had shredded. Reagan would subsequently excuse these memory lapses at a press conference by asking "everybody who can remember what they were doing on August 8, 1985" to "raise your hands" — as if approving arms sales to Iran were a minor decision quite easily forgotten.

The commission's big break came with the discovery of PROFS, the computer mail system North and Poindexter had frequently used to communi-

cate. Although North had erased most of the incriminating files, he was unaware of a backup security system that had preserved intact copies of most of the memos.

While detailing Iran-contra in its report of February 26, 1987, the Tower Commission absolved Reagan of knowledge of the diversion of funds but took special pains to hold him responsible for the scandal and to upbraid him for his severely lax management style. Reagan may never have read the report, for he continued to insist that not one shred of evidence had ever explained who had raised the price of weapons sold to Iran, who had got that money, or where it had gone, even though the report was quite explicit on these matters.

During joint congressional committee hearings on Iran-contra, North stoutly defended his actions and, appealing to America's patriotic sentiments, became the hero Reagan had said he was. Subsequent speaking engagements earned North as much

John Nields, Jr. (left), special counsel for the House panel probing the Iran-contra affair, confers with Arthur Liman, special counsel for the Senate panel. As the revelations of the Iran-contra affair became known, much doubt was cast on the wisdom of President Reagan's hands-off management style.

as $25,000 each, but Congress remained unconvinced, and a bipartisan majority of the congressional investigating committee concluded that President Reagan had violated his oath of office.

Looking for someone to blame — in hopes of clearing her husband's name — Nancy Reagan focused on Donald Regan, whom she had disliked at least since the summer of 1985, when she had found him pushy and obnoxious during Reagan's recovery from cancer surgery. Nancy Reagan pressured her husband to fire Donald Regan and enlisted Michael Deaver's aid in the effort. But Reagan liked Regan — perhaps because Regan greeted the president each day with a joke. By early 1987, news of Regan's feud with Mrs. Reagan was reported by the *New York Times* and the *Washington Post*. As pressure and bad publicity mounted, Regan prepared his resignation. But even before he could deliver it on February 27, Howard Baker — a former senator and a highly regarded moderate Republican who had distinguished himself during the Watergate investigations—was announced as his replacement.

A federal grand jury would eventually indict North, Poindexter, Secord, and Hakim for conspiracy to defraud the government and steal government property, among other crimes. Carl Channell would plead guilty to conspiring to defraud the government of taxes. McFarlane would plead guilty to four counts of withholding information from Congress, reduced charges received for agreeing to testify against North. Poindexter would also be indicted for his involvement in the scandal.

Perhaps the best analogue for what was happening to the Reagan administration can be found in the fate of the U.S. space program during the Reagan years. On April 12, 1981, the first reusable spacecraft, the space shuttle *Columbia*, had been launched successfully, and the future looked bright. The future looked even brighter on June 18, 1983, when Sally Ride became the first American woman in space. But on the cold day of January 28, 1986, the space shuttle *Challenger* exploded within minutes of its launch, killing all seven crew members instantly — including a schoolteacher who had been added to the mission to encourage American schoolchildren to become more interested in space flight. Morton Thiokol — the corporation responsible for the O-ring that had failed because of the cold and caused the shuttle's solid fuel to burn out of control — and officials at the National Aeronautics and Space Administration (NASA) knew better than to risk the flight in such inclement weather, but under public and administrative pressure, they went ahead with the mission despite the apparent danger. After the *Challenger* disaster, America's space program was put on hold indefinitely.

While Reagan languished as badly as the space program, the 100th Congress seized the initiative. Beginning in early 1987, it passed an extension of the Clean Water Act, banned federal funds for institutions guilty of discrimination, passed a plant-closing bill requiring employers to give affected employees 60 days notification, enacted fair housing and welfare reform, provided aid to the homeless, expanded the food stamp program, sought to protect Americans from financial ruin due to catastrophic illness, and increased funding for elementary and secondary education — in other words, tried to repair much of the damage caused to the body politic by Reagan's administration. All of these bills were passed over Reagan's objections. He vetoed several of the bills, but Congress overrode his vetoes.

In the summer of 1987, Reagan had another opportunity to influence the Supreme Court's direction when Lewis Powell, for the most part not a conservative, retired. Because Supreme Court appointments are for life, this was an opportunity for Reagan to influence Court decisions for decades to come by appointing another conservative to the bench. But he stumbled badly. Reagan's first nominee, district court judge and Yale University professor Robert Bork — whose views might well have proved detrimental to civil rights, the right to privacy, and free speech — was repudiated by the Senate after acrimonious public hearings. Reagan's

In an attempt to secure a conservative judiciary for years to come, Reagan nominated Judge Robert H. Bork to the Supreme Court in 1987. Because of his strong belief in an interpretation of the Constitution based on the "original intent" of its framers that would strictly limit the role of the Court, Bork was not confirmed by the Senate.

second nominee, Douglas Ginsburg — who Reagan claimed was every bit as conservative as Bork — was forced to withdraw his nomination after it was learned that he had smoked marijuana not only in youth but as a member of the Harvard Law School faculty. The third nominee, Anthony Kennedy, was finally confirmed. Kennedy too was a conservative, but the California law professor was nowhere near as objectionable to liberals as Bork and Ginsburg had been.

Adding insult to injury, the economy — which had continued to perform splendidly even during Iran-contra — received a serious blow in October 1987 in the form of a stock market crash. The collapse of stock prices was even more dramatic than that of the crash of 1929, which had signaled the onset of the Great Depression.

Searching for an issue with which to restore the Reagan presidency, Chief of Staff Baker seized on U.S.-Soviet relations. Long-stalled arms control negotiations had gotten back on track in the spring of 1985 — after Soviet leader Yuri Andropov's successor, Konstantin Chernenko, died on March 10 — when the new Soviet premier, Gorbachev, and Reagan's men drafted an arms control agreement the two leaders were able to sign that November in Geneva. Even if Reagan and Gorbachev had quarreled in Reykjavík in October 1986, the conditions that had caused them almost to eliminate all ballistic missiles still existed. Something could be done.

The first break came in February 1987, when the Soviets agreed to separate intermediate-range missile discussions from talks on SDI. By the end of October, negotiators were close enough to agreement for Gorbachev to schedule a visit to Washington in early December, and before Gorbachev arrived, a document banning all intermediate-range and some shorter-range missiles was ready for signing. Perhaps more important, Reagan and Gorbachev agreed during the summit to meet again in Moscow the following spring.

That Ronald Reagan would willingly fly to the Soviet capital of Moscow on a friendly mission was the

To those of us who remember the postwar era, all of this is cause for shaking the head in wonder. Imagine, the President of the United States and the General Secretary of the Soviet Union walking together in Red Square, talking about a growing personal friendship.
—RONALD REAGAN
on meeting with
Mikhail Gorbachev

Soviet leader Gorbachev and President Reagan sign the Intermediate-range Nuclear Forces (INF) treaty at the White House in 1987. The agreement, a major achievement of the Reagan administration in the area of foreign affairs, banned all intermediate and some short-range missiles.

one undertaking no one would have predicted when Reagan first took office. In any event, the Moscow summit was low-key. A few agreements on minor issues — such as nuclear-testing procedures, fishing rights, and student and cultural exchanges — were signed. Reagan scored propaganda points by speaking out on religious and political freedom and meeting with Soviet dissidents.

More than anything, the Moscow summit was the ultimate photo opportunity. At the end of his visit, during a walk through Red Square, Reagan spontaneously put his arm around his host's shoulder. Gorbachev spotted a small child in the crowd and asked her to "shake hands with Grandfather Reagan." As Reagan lifted and hugged the child, he might well have hoped that this image of him was the one Americans would remember.

8

Farewell Tour

When Vice-president Bush ran for president as the Republican nominee in 1988, he clearly had learned from his mentor. Taking lessons to lower his voice and control his wayward gestures, he presented a campaign so devoid of substance, even Ronald Reagan may have marvelled. Reagan's presidency was a triumph of image over action, of appearance over reality, and so was Bush's campaign. The Democratic challenger, Massachusetts governor Michael Dukakis, never understood the primacy of the television bite — the nugget of self-presentation that plays well on the nightly newscasts — and therefore never stood a chance.

Long before the election, Mrs. Reagan had begun shipping the Reagans' personal possessions to yet another new home purchased for them, in Bel-Air, California. The purchase money was provided mostly by anonymous donors, each of whom had contributed $150,000. As during their Sacramento days, the Reagans rented the house.

> With Reagan, the perfection of the pretense lies in the fact that he does not know he is pretending. . . . He is the sincerest claimant to a heritage that never existed, a perfect blend of an authentic America he grew up in and of that America's own fables about its past.
> —GARY WILLS
> Reagan biographer

As the Reagan era draws to a close, President-elect George Bush, President Reagan, and Soviet leader Gorbachev visit New York in December 1988. Bush smeared his Democratic opponent, Massachusetts governor Michael Dukakis, with a negative media campaign that many pundits considered one of the low points in the history of American politics.

Former president Reagan lectures to more than 11,000 students at Arizona State University on March 20, 1989. After he left the White House, Reagan hit the lecture circuit, charging between $30,000 and $50,000 per speech, and signed a $5 million contract to publish his memoirs with Simon & Schuster.

The ex-president and his wife had plenty of money but were about to make a lot more. Publishers Simon & Schuster purchased a volume of selected speeches and Reagan's yet-unwritten memoirs for more than $5 million. Reagan also intended a return to the lecture circuit, charging $30,000 to $50,000 a speech. For a 2-day visit to Japan, the former president would earn $2 million, mostly to finance a library to house his presidential papers.

On May 4, 1989, Oliver North was convicted of destroying government documents, misleading Congress, and accepting an "illegal gratuity" — a $13,800 home security system paid for by Richard

Secord. Contributors to his defense fund donated hundreds of thousands of dollars, and 52 percent of the public thought he should be pardoned, but Judge Gerhard Gesell gave North a 3-year suspended sentence, put him on a 2-year probation, ordered him to devote 1,200 hours to community drug rehabilitation programs, and fined him $150,000. Many believed that Reagan, not North, should have been tried.

Reagan had been the first president since Eisenhower to complete two terms in office — a triumph in itself. By playing the role of president extremely well, he had restored to the office a grandeur it had long lacked. Still, in other ways he had failed miserably. In two terms he was not able to accomplish his goals of restoring prayer in public schools, banning abortion, passing a constitutional amendment mandating a balanced budget, and obtaining the line-item veto (with which a president could eliminate items from congressionally approved budgets).

A homeless man, who spent the night on a park bench across the street from the White House, wakes up to find that "it's morning in America." Though Reaganomics created the yuppie (young urban professional) phenomenon and thus the appearance of national prosperity, many middle- and lower-middle-class Americans experienced greater economic pressures during the Reagan years.

This sculpture incorporating a huge picture of Ronald Reagan was part of an open-air exhibit called "Art on the Beach" at New York City's Battery Park during the mid-1980s. The Reagan years saw severe cuts in federal funding for the arts and education.

Though he had promised in his campaign rhetoric to eliminate federal deficits, he presided over the creation of deficits larger than those of all his predecessors combined. He left behind a weakened dollar and a struggling economy, reflected in the increase of homeless and jobless Americans since 1980.

Two of the worst scandals of the Reagan administration were only uncovered after Reagan left office. The Department of Housing and Urban Development was revealed as a cesspool of fraud, theft, patronage, and favoritism, costing taxpayers hundreds of millions of dollars. The collapse of the savings and loan industry — due to inadequate regulation, CIA manipulation, and organized crime infiltration — would result in a massive federal bailout, with estimates running at more than $500 billion, a cost ultimately passed on to American taxpayers.

The Reagan deficit would diminish economic prospects for generations to come, the Reagan administration's exploitation of the enviroment to further business interests despoiled and poisoned the land and the air, and the Reagan record on civil rights left a legacy of escalating racial antagonism and even racial violence. His administration had also been corrupt beyond measure. No wonder a poll in 1990 showed Reagan was even less popular than Jimmy Carter when he left office.

On February 16 and 17, 1990, Reagan earned the dubious distinction of becoming the first American president required to testify in criminal proceedings concerning his administration. In a dismal and dispiriting performance, the former president spent eight hours answering questions about Iran-contra for the trial of John Poindexter. Profoundly ignorant of what had happened in his White House, Reagan had to answer "I don't know" or "I don't remember" so often that even he was embarrassed. In defense of his failed memory, he offered statisticians' estimates that he had met an average of 80 people a day every day of his presidency, almost 250,000 people. Does that explain his inability to identify a photograph of his chairman of the Joint Chiefs of Staff or excuse his continuing insistence that he had still seen no evidence suggesting that the diversion of funds from Iran to the contras ever happened? Would it be charitable to reflect that Reagan was then 79 years old and had suffered a postpresidential riding accident requiring the removal of fluid from his brain?

Assessments of the Reagan presidency began before he left office and were provided by a startling number of books written by former aides: Alexander Haig's *Caveat*, David Stockman's *The Triumph of Politics*, Michael Deaver's *Behind the Scenes*, Press Secretary Larry Speakes's *Speaking Out*, and Donald Regan's *For the Record*, among others. Nancy Reagan offered her version of the record in *My Turn*. Even her astrologer, Joan Quigley, weighed in with a book touting her own importance in the conduct of White House affairs during the Reagan admin-

Money rather than service has been the theme of this ex-President. In February [1990] he spent an hour at a Florida convention of hamburger franchise operators and collected $60,000.
—ANTHONY LEWIS
New York Times columnist

The Reagans relax on their 688-acre mountain ranch near Santa Barbara, California. From the obscurity of small-town Illinois to the White House, Reagan was the epitome of American determination and optimism. Regardless of whether his conservative revolution continues beyond the 1990s, Reagan will be remembered for his role in making many Americans feel good about America.

istration. In her book *What Does Joan Say?*, Quigley claimed that the Reagans consulted her on numerous occasions regarding political decisions.

The Reagan era will no doubt be the subject of debate for many decades to come. The American public is still, in the words of "Doonesbury" cartoonist Garry Trudeau, *In Search of Reagan's Brain* and probably will be for some time. Perhaps Reagan's memoirs will shed some new light on the man who led, in fact came to symbolize, America's conservative revolution of the 1980s. More likely, they will constitute as polished a performance as any in his lifetime, leaving us still wondering about the man behind the role.

We who are his contemporaries cannot say with certainty whether or not Ronald Reagan was a great president. Such a determination will require historical distance, the unfolding of time, the completion of the story. Still, in the post–Reagan era the words of John Adams, one of the Founding Fathers of the United States of America and the country's second president, might need updating. Of our first president, George Washington, Adams said, "If he was not the greatest president, he was the best actor in the presidency we have ever had." Now that the world has witnessed the rise of "the Gipper" to the nation's highest office, a new role player may hold that distinction.

Further Reading

Cannon, Lou. *Reagan.* New York: Putnam, 1982.

Deaver, Michael K., with Mickey Herskowitz. *Behind the Scenes.* New York: Morrow, 1987.

Ehrenreich, Barbara. *The Worst Years of Our Lives: Irreverent Notes from a Decade of Greed.* New York: Pantheon Books, 1990.

Karp, Walter. *Liberty Under Siege: American Politics 1976–1988.* New York: Henry Holt, 1988.

Leamer, Laurence. *Make-believe: The Story of Ron and Nancy Reagan.* New York: Harper & Row, 1983.

Leighton, Frances Spatz. *The Search for the Real Nancy Reagan.* New York: Macmillan, 1987.

Mandelbaum, Michael, and Strobe Talbott. *Reagan and Gorbachev.* New York: Vintage Books, 1987.

Mayer, Jane, and Doyle McManus. *Landslide: The Unmaking of the President, 1984–1988.* Boston: Houghton Mifflin, 1988.

Moynihan, Daniel Patrick. *Came the Revolution: Argument in the Reagan Era.* San Diego: Harcourt Brace Jovanovich, 1988.

Reagan, Nancy. *My Turn.* New York: Harper & Row, 1989.

Reagan, Ronald. *An American Life: Ronald Reagan, the Autobiography.* New York: Simon & Schuster, 1990.

Reagan, Ronald, and Richard G. Hubler. *Where's the Rest of Me?* New York: Duell, Sloan, Pearce, 1965.

Regan, Donald T. *For the Record: From Wall Street to Washington.* San Diego: Harcourt Brace Jovanovich, 1988.

Schieffer, Bob, and Gary Paul Gates. *The Acting President.* New York: Dutton, 1989.

Smith, David, and Melinda Gebbie. *Reagan for Beginners.* London: Writers and Readers Publishing, 1984.

Stockman, David A. *The Triumph of Politics: Why the Reagan Revolution Failed.* New York: Harper & Row, 1986.

Wills, Garry. *Reagan's America: Innocents at Home.* Garden City, NY: Doubleday, 1987.

Chronology

Feb. 6, 1911	Born Ronald Wilson Reagan in Tampico, Illinois
1928	Enrolls at Eureka College
1933	Broadcasts baseball games for radio station WOC in Davenport, Iowa
Jan. 1940	Marries actress Jane Wyman
1940	Stars in *Knute Rockne, All American*
1946	Appointed president of the Screen Actors Guild
1947	Testifies before House Un-American Activities Committee; elected president of the Screen Actors Guild (first of five times)
June 1949	Divorces Jane Wyman
1951	Stars in *Bedtime for Bonzo*
March 1952	Marries Nancy Davis
1954	Becomes corporate spokesman for General Electric Company
1957	Stars in final feature film, *Hellcats of the Navy*
1965	Writes autobiography, *Where's the Rest of Me?*
1966	Elected governor of California
1968	First campaign for the presidency
1970	Reelected governor
1976	Second campaign for the presidency
1980	Elected 40th president of the United States
1981	Wounded during assassination attempt by John David Hinckley; fires striking air traffic controllers; appoints Sandra Day O'Connor to the Supreme Court
1983	Proposes Strategic Defense Initiative, the "Star Wars" military defense system; 241 soldiers murdered in terrorist bombing of U.S. Marine barracks in Beirut; United States forces invade Grenada
1984	Reagan reelected president
1985	Visits cemetery in Bitburg, Germany, where Nazi soldiers are buried; approves arms sale to Iran; first meeting with Mikhail Gorbachev
1986	Space shuttle *Challenger* explodes; Reagan orders bombing of Libya; appoints William Rehnquist chief justice of the United States and Antonin Scalia associate justice of the Supreme Court; Iran-contra scandal first revealed
1987	Tower Commission report issued on Iran-contra; Anthony Kennedy appointed to the Supreme Court after Robert Bork and Douglas Ginsburg are rejected; Reagan-Gorbachev summit in Washington
1988	Oliver North, John Poindexter, Richard Secord, and Albert Hakim indicted in Iran-contra affair; Reagan-Gorbachev summit in Moscow; George Bush elected president
1989	Reagan signs contract with Simon & Schuster for speeches and memoirs; receives $2 million for appearance in Japan
1990	Gives testimony in Poindexter trial

Index

Renée Schwartzberg is a New York–based novelist, playwright, director, and actor, with a special interest in the history of film and theater. A graduate of Brown University, she has written several biographies for young adults.

Arthur M. Schlesinger, jr., taught history at Harvard for many years and is currently Albert Schweitzer Professor of the Humanities at City University of New York. He is the author of numerous highly praised works in American history and has twice been awarded the Pulitzer Prize. He served in the White House as special assistant to Presidents Kennedy and Johnson.